Ethics in Tirukkuṟaḷ and Ācārakkōvai

Ethics in Tirukkuṟaḷ and Ācārakkōvai

Govindaswamy Rajagopal

Ethics in Tirukkuṟaḷ and Ācārakkōvai

Govindaswamy Rajagopal
Professor of Tamil
Department of Indian Languages and Literary Studies
University of Delhi, Delhi-110 007

Email: grajagopaldu@gmail.com

Published by
Pharos Books Pvt. Ltd.,
Plot No. 63, First Floor, Pandav Nagar, Delhi-110092

First published in 2016 with the title
Etiquette and Ethos: Ethics in Tirukkuṟaḷ and Ācārakkōvai
by
Sun International Publishers,
PG-105, Possangipur, Janakpuri, New Delhi-110058

PB ISBN: 978-93-67001-40-0
HB ISBN: 978-93-67003-62-6
eISBN: 978-93-67003-69-5

Dedicated to

(Late) Prof. S. Ulaganathan,
a fine human being, a beloved teacher
and an inspirational guide and philosopher

Contents

Acknowledgement

This book, comprising three essays, is an attempt to illustrate some primary virtues and some unique recurring Tamiḻ terms, viz. *cānṟōṉ* (a noble man), *nōkku* (the sight of love), *naṭpu* (love, i.e., the sexual relationship), *virundu* (novelty), *naṉṟi* (a good deed), and *nāṟṟam* (fragrance) rendered in the universally acclaimed ethical treatise *Tirukkuṟaḷ* and injunctions of Vedic codes and practices pronounced in *Ācārakkōvai*, an exceptional ethical work of the post-Sangam period (*c.* 250–600 CE).

This small book would not have seen the light of the day, without the kind support of several people. First of all, I wish to convey my heartfelt gratitude to the authorities of the University of Delhi, espccially to **Prof. Malashri Lal**, former Chairperson and the members of the Research Council, who provided me with the required financial aid under the scheme of Research and Development Grant 2015–16, which ultimately paved the way for the publication of this book.

My warm regards are due to **Prof. R. Sri Hari** (General Editor), and my guru (late) **Prof. Pon. Sourirajan** and **Prof. V. Gopalakrishna** (Editors), Dravidian University, Kuppam, Andhra Pradesh, who were kind enough then to include and publish my article titled "Didactic Literature in Tamiḻ: A Genre for Social Cause" in the book titled *Major Genres and Trends in Dravidian Literature (Classical)*, published in 2003.

And I sincerely thank **Dato' Seri Dr. S. Samyvellu**, the Chairman and **Dr. N. Kanthasamy**, General Secretary, *9th International Conference–Seminar on Tamiḻ Studies*, who extended me an invitation to present my paper titled "Deciphering the Peculiar Cultural Significance of Some Terms in Tirukkuṟaḷ" in the aforesaid International Conference, held between 29th January–1st February 2015, at the University of Malaya, Kuala Lumpur, Malaysia.

Also, I wish to extend my earnest gratitude to the authorities of the Central Institute of Classical Tamil, Chennai, to the Principal, P.S.G.R. Krishanammal College for Women, Coimbatore, Tamil Nadu and to the Organizing Committee members of the National Conference on "Padiṉeṉ Kīḻkkaṇakku Nūlgaḷil Kaḍamaigaḷum Urimaigaḷum" ("Tamil Didactic Literary Works: Duties and Rights"), held at Coimbatore during 11–13, February 2010, in which I presented a paper in Tamil titled "Uṟakkam Mudal Tuṟakkam Varai: Ācāra–Aṉācāraṅgaḷ" ("From Sleeping to Salvation: Ethical Codes and Evil Deeds").

My heartfelt thanks to **Prof. Vanathu Antoni**, former Senior Fellow in our department, who carefully fine-tuned the language of the manuscript with his professional expertise. Grateful to my erstwhile PhD Research Fellow, **Dr. Shruti Bhushan,** for her useful comments and meaningful suggestions in making the manuscript perfect in every sense. My special thanks to **Mrs. Neeharika Singh Lodhi,** my erstwhile M.Phil. Research Fellow, for re-publishing this book gracefully.

I would like to offer my sincere gratitude to the (late) **'Pulavar' R. Vishwanathan**, an eminent scholar on Tirukkuṟaḷ, for rendering an erudite "Foreword" to this book, amidst his fatigued health issues and pressing household obligations. I sincerely acknowledge the constant support extended by my son, **R. Ilamparidi** (an Advocate-on-Record before the Hon'ble Supreme Court of India), and the continual backing offered by my wife, **Dr. Neelakandan Rajeswari** who bore all the inconveniences of managing household responsibilities.

15 May 2025   Govindaswamy Rajagopal

Foreword

Tamil, one of the most ancient languages still thriving today, has an enviable body of world-class literature. Time and again, reading and re-reading its universally acclaimed didactic work *Tirukkuṟaḷ*, the classical epics, viz. *Cilappatikāram* and *Kamba Rāmāyaṇam* and ever moving powerful poems of 'Mahakavi' Subramaniya Bharati, in fact, never fail to amuse and impart immeasurable insights to me on myriad subjects. Surely, one can acquire so much aesthetic pleasure, delightful truths and high ethical values from these brilliant literary pieces. Plentiful research studies, of course with divergent agendas, are being systematically conducted on almost all Tamil literary texts since colonial period. Now, here is a book authored by Govindaswamy Rajagopal, one of my acquaintances of nearly three decades, to be added to the exciting repository of Tamil research studies.

This book, comprising three essays—two on *Tirukkuṟaḷ* and one on *Ācārakkōvai*—is a fascinating critical study. As we are aware, the *Tirukkuṟaḷ* is "a Scripture of Maxims of Truth" meant for everyone to be adhered to practically. The book, a mine of facts, is a treatise of ethical values suitable for everyone, whether kings, ministers, soldiers, husbands, wives, parents, children and others. Though it sounds strange, it is also an aesthetic guidebook for lovers too. The other text *Ācārakkōvai* is an exceptional Tamil didactic work which religiously speaks of a volume of Vedic codes and practices. It is a slender but effective manual for traditional people who are familiar with decrees fond observances endorsed by age-old Vedic Hinduism. Contents of these ethical works clearly spell out their true nature and stature for themselves. While the former scripture profoundly discusses every aspect of human welfare, the latter instinctively dialogues on almost all canons and ritual entities concerned largely with a particular section or a community of humanity.

In the first chapter titled "Virtues in Tirukkuṟaḷ and Other Tamil Didactic Works: A Bird's Eye View," the author Rajagopal, though not elaborately yet diligently, discusses certain core ethics endorsed by Tiruvaḷḷuvar. He has adeptly shown that the frequent wars among the traditional rulers of Tamil Nadu, viz. Cēra, Cōḻa, and Pāṇḍiya, their subsequent loss of political power to the intruders Kalabhras (of Karnataka), increasing influence of North over Tamil country and the internal uncertainty prevailing in post-Sangam age (*c.* 200–600 CE)—all these factors have contributed to the advent of *Tirukkuṟaḷ* as an ethical guide for people on righteous path.

Then, the author candidly quoted Tiruvaḷḷuvar's definition about *aṟam* (virtue) saying, "Whatever is done with a spotless mind is *aṟam* (virtue); all else is vain show" (*TKḶ* 44). While rightly illustrating how Tiruvaḷḷuvar emphasizes the importance of household life over ascetic existence, the author amply illustrates the content of a couplet: "A householder who, not swerving from virtue, helps the ascetic in his way endures more than those who endure penance" (*TKḶ* 48). Rajagopal justly opines that Tiruvaḷḷuvar seems to have been influenced largely by the tenets of Jainism and Buddhism. So, he candidly observes that the universal moral preacher earnestly discourses a volume of ethics for men to abstain themselves from killing beings and meat-eating, staying away from boozing and gambling, keeping away from stealing, lying and infidelity and so on. Later, at the end of the chapter, the author pertinently highlighted some fine virtues related to learning, friendship, chastity, wealth, hospitality, etc., as they have been illustrated in other Tamil didactic works.

The second chapter titled "Familiar Terms and Unfamiliar Connotations: Cultural Overtones in Tirukkuṟaḷ" is an in-depth textual study on certain unique Tamil terms, viz. *cānṟōn* (a noble man), *nōkku* (the sight of love), *naṭpu* (love, i.e., the sexual relationship), *virundu* (novelty), *naṉri* (a good deed), and *nāṟṟam* (fragrance) as rendered in the classical Sangam works and *Tirukkuṟaḷ*. The author shows with good examples how the peculiar term *cānṟōr* originally meant "men of heroic deeds" in the Sangam age which later came to denote "the learned" and "the men of noble characters" in *Tirukkuṟaḷ* days. The author then discourses thoughtfully on the etymological and semantic aspects of other terms too amusingly. Interestingly, he has dealt with the term *nōkku* and establishes pertinently its original meaning, i.e., "the sight of love." He ably illustrated its principal connotation by employing the following analogy: *"Pār-Kāṇ-Nōkku"* ("See-View-Look"). In a similar manner, the author dealt with the remaining terms too and thereby appropriately elucidated their primary meanings. In his precise analysis, *naṭpu* denotes "love," i.e., the sexual relationship found naturally between mature male and female but not the usual friendship between people of same sex; *virundu*, novelty/newness/unknown people but not guest or feast; *naṉri*, good deed or fine actions but not gratefulness/gratitude; *nāṟṟam*, fine fragrance/good smell but not bad or rotten smell, the prevailing connotations of these terms at present. The author effectively showed how some commentators and translators failed to capture exact meanings of these terms contextually by taking their current meanings wrongly into consideration. To establish the early meanings of the aforesaid recurring terms, Rajagopal meticulously cited a volume of Sangam poems and a number of couplets from *Tirukkuṟaḷ* to substantiate his impressive proposition.

The third chapter titled "From Sleeping to Salvation: Vedic Codes and Practices" is a scholarly study of Brāhmāṇic injunctions pronounced in the didactic text *Ācārakkōvai*. It poignantly deliberates on all codes of conduct—that people are supposed to follow in their personal (home) and societal (public) lives. To my knowledge, this study is the first attempt which critically as well as exhaustively analyzes *Ācārakkōvai*, a unique Tamil ethical text. The author's approach to this treatise of Vedic *Dharmaśāstra* is, indeed, heartening and commendable. He dealt with the verses of this didactic work very systematically. And methodically he analyzed customary behaviours and ritual observances that any traditional person needs to adhere to in his/her daily life—from dawn to dusk, from awakening to sleeping, and from eating to excreting.

Rajagopal credibly cited a number of *smrtis* (pronouncements) of Manu and decrees of others in the quest for establishing the religious influence of North over South (Tamil Nadu) in the earlier days. While explaining the valid reasons that operate in the dictums of certain Vedic codes and practices, the author points out irrationality and non-adaptability of certain observances and rituals in day-to-day life of the common man. His humorous disagreements in some contexts are quite intriguing.

This extensive but erudite essay at the end rightly concludes saying: "Essentially, everyone should adhere genuinely to the core etiquette and ethos of their society wherein they live for his/her happiness and that of fellow beings. Perhaps, in the quest for shepherding humans in the righteous path, the *Dharmaśāstras* and *Ācārakkōvai* reiterate the […] abstract forts, viz. 'heaven' and 'hell' by employing the typical strategy of reward or punishment to people's virtuous conducts and evil deeds respectively."

By and large, the sincere academic endeavour conducted by Rajagopal, indeed, merits appreciation. I congratulate him wholeheartedly on coming out with such thought-provoking essays. I hope this intense study will fascinate people who are interested in knowing different ethical codes and conducts, beliefs and practices that were postulated in the post-Sangam era.

(Late) 'Pulavar' R. Vishwanathan
A–3C, DDA Flats
Munirka, New Delhi-110 067

Preface

Tamil, an ancient language which flourished well before the arrival of Jesus Christ, is the first vernacular duly declared as a classical language by the Union Government of India on 12th October 2004. It has an envious repertoire of a rich array of grammatical and literary masterpieces. Its *Tolkāppiyam* (*c.* 300 BCE), the earliest grammatical treatise, the primary anthologies, viz. *Eṭṭuttogai* (Eight Anthologies) and *Pattup-pāṭṭu* (Ten Idylls) collectively known as "Sangam Literature" (*c.* 200 BCE–200 CE) comprising 2,381 lyrics, *Tirukkuṟaḷ* (*c.* 250 CE), "the Universal Tamiḻ Scripture," and *Cilappa-digāram* (*c.* 300 CE), the first Tamiḻ epic, in fact, are no longer confined to Tamiḻ territory but have become part of the world's literary heritage.

As we are aware, every language or linguistic community has its own distinct ethnic culture with different customs, ethos, ethics, codes and conducts, rules and regulations developed and cherished for years. Being an independent and a distinctive language of India, Tamiḻ has a rich cultural heritage spanning a period of over 2300 years. As Tamiḻ ethnicity historically belonged to 'Heroic Age' (*c.* 3000 BCE–300 CE), the ethnic group upheld both *aham* ("interior"/"love sentiments") and *puṟam* ("exterior actions"/"heroic values") equally, as their two eyes. As the monarchical era of kings held absolute power, often accompanied by atrocities and ceaseless battles/wars over wealth and territory, there were chaotic and terrible situations prevailing in the country. So, in the much-disturbed condition, didactic poets like Tiruvaḷḷuvar penned how life should be lived and what sort of moral percepts and codes and conducts should govern it. Also, the increasing influence of North over South in general, and over Tamil̲ country in particular during the post-Sangam period contributed much to the development of Didactic literature in Tamil̲. Thereby a versifier named Kayattūr Peruvāyin̲ Muḷḷiyār brought out a unique ethical text called *Ācārakkōvai*, which wholly endorses the Vedic codes and practices to Tamil̲s.

Obviously, all literary creations including essays on literary themes, either implicitly or explicitly, discuss some cultural aspects of a given language of ethnicity. In a literary text, even a simple or ordinary word, besides its literal or primary meaning, may invoke a 'unique cultural connotation' of an ethnic group. To unveil its *hidden meaning*, one needs to probe or decode the given word contextually rather than just literally. In this endeavour, the period in which the literary text is produced is paramount for comprehending its "cultural poetics."

It is well known that humans are social beings. Subsequently, the manner/conduct/behaviour of one's 'inner-self' may be generally termed as "culture." The term refers to a way of life of a group of people, cumulative deposit of their knowledge, experience, beliefs, values, attitudes, meanings, hierarchies, religion, notion of time, roles, spatial relations, concepts of the universe, and material objects and possessions acquired by a group of people in the course of generations through individual and group striving. Culture in its broadest sense is the cultivated behaviour, that is the totality of the person's learned, accumulated experience, which is socially transmitted, or more briefly, behaviour through social learning. Contrary to this, the actions or reflections of man's 'outer-self' (body/physique) may be termed as "civilization." Neither an individual's nor ethnicity's culture and civilization remain unchanged forever. Naturally, they tend to change/

transform in due course of time according to the necessity of situations. A person who acts in a certain manner at a particular time may experience changes in both 'inner emotions' and 'outer conducts.' The socio-political-economic-religious conditions of a given period do act as factors behind his/her culture and civilization. The vicissitudes and fluctuations that influence the 'inner' and 'outer-selves' of a person/an ethnicity can be termed as "cultural mobility."

Considering the universally acclaimed *Tirukkuṟaḷ* as the epitome of ancient Tamiḻs' ethics, and the unique didactic text called *Ācārakkōvai* as the sole illustration of Brāhmaṇism preaching every code and conduct of Vedic creed, the essays in the present book try to decipher some unique terms and certain Vedic codes and practices endorsed therein. The first essay titled "Virtues in Tirukkuṟaḷ and Other Tamiḻ Didactic Works – A Bird's Eye View," though not exhaustive, discusses in detail some major virtues and some evil deeds stated in *Tirukkuṟaḷ, Nālaḍiyār, Paḻamoḻi Nāṉūṟu, Ācārakkōvai, Ciṟupañcamūlam,* etc. The second essay titled "Familiar Terms and Unfamiliar Connotations: Cultural Overtones in Tirukkuṟaḷ" expressly deliberates thoroughly on certain unique terms such as *cāṉṟōr* (a noble man), *nōkku* (the sight of love), *naṭpu* (love, i.e., the sexual relationship), *virundu* (novelty), *naṉṟi* (a good deed), and *nāṟṟam* (fragrance) as rendered in the classical Sangam works and *Tirukkuṟaḷ*—the specific recurring terms of cultural significance. These terms nonetheless effectively reflect the socio-political-religious-cultural life of the Tamiḻs of the preceding era. By expounding the chronological account of the origin and development of these peculiar terms in the Sangam poems and more specifically in *Tirukkuṟaḷ*, the essay brings forth the cultural mobility or shift that has taken place in the lives of Tamiḻs. The third essay titled "From Sleeping to Salvation: Vedic Codes and Practices" intensely discourses on the Brāhmaṇic injunctions pronounced in the didactic text *Ācārakkōvai*. It poignantly deliberates on all codes and conducts—that one needs to adhere sincerely to in his/her inner (home) and outer (public) spheres—as prescribed by the versifier Kayattūr Peruvāyiṉ Muḷḷiyār. The study, though not comprehensive, it diligently discusses certain predominant virtues and Vedic codes and practices illustrated in *Tirukkuṟaḷ*, and other Tamiḻ didactic works.

I hope these essays will inspire renewed interest in revisiting the entire corpus of Tamiḻ didactic texts in terms of their cultural connotations and ritual codes and practices prescribed to Tamiḻs of bygone era.

15 May 2025   Govindaswamy Rajagopal

Abbreviations

ĀK	=	*Ācārakkōvai*
ANU	=	*Ahanāṉūṟu*
BCE	=	Before Christ Era
c.	=	*circa* means "approximately"
CE	=	Christ Era
Cf.	=	*Confer* < *Conferre* means "compare" or "see also"
comm.	=	commentary/commentator
ed.	=	editor/edition
eds.	=	editors
e.g.	=	*exempli gratia* means "for example"
et al.	=	*et alii* means "and others"
etc.	=	*et cetera* means "and other things," or "and so forth"
Ibid.	=	*Ibidem* means "in the same place"
i.e.	=	*id est* means "that is"
KLT	=	*Kalittogai*
KRT	=	*Kuṟuntogai*
NDR	=	*Nāladiyār*
NRI	=	*Naṟṟiṇai*
Op. cit.	=	*Opere citato* means "in the work cited"
p.	=	page
pp.	=	pages
PPL	=	*Paripāḍal*
PNU	=	*Puṟanāṉūṟu*
Pub.	=	Publisher
Rpt.	=	Reprint
Skt.	=	Sanskrit
tr.	=	translation/translator
trs.	=	translators
TKḶ	=	*Tirukkuṟaḷ*
TVR	=	Tiruvaḷḷuvar
viz.	=	namely

Chapter – One

Virtues in Tirukkuṟaḷ and Other Tamiḻ Didactic Works: A Bird's Eye View*

Literature, like any other art form, has a specific role to play in society. Any piece of literature serves dual purposes: to entertain and to instruct humanity. While entertaining, literature would also impart a specific message to society. Besides, a literary text may serve several functions such as cognitive, expressive, persuasive, aesthetic and so on. A text dominated by persuasion is termed *didactic*, while one with a prevailing aesthetic function is considered *literature* proper, even though it also conveys a message indirectly. The term *didactic* is a derivative of the Greek root *didaktikos* (*dedasko* = teach) meaning "apt at teaching."[1] As such, literature that intends primarily to teach humans, could be called "Didactic Literature." Incidentally, the seeds of didactic literature can be noticed right from the ancient Tamiḻ poems popularly known as "Sangam literature" (*c.* 200 BCE–200 CE). Through the modes of *aham* (> *akam*, "love poems") and *puṟam* poems (other than love themes such as polity, war, munificence, etc.), the poets did administer a volume of morals, both directly and indirectly through the dramatis personae and historical characters in keeping with the poetic tradition. Out of these two modes, the *puṟam* poems, being lyrical, have a good deal of opportunities to instruct, while keeping the poetic function dominant. Didactic tone, though rarely found in *aham* poems, is seen often in the *pālai* (parched wasteland region signifying the 'separation') love poems. A newly married young husband intends to go abroad to earn and lead a comfortable life. Having come to know of his mind, *tōḻi* (confidante) tries to dissuade him from taking such a painful mission for material life. She eloquently makes him understand that when one is blessed with youth and requited love, what other good is there for such a one to expect from wealth except living with his wife in an inseparable union that is true living (*Kalittogai* 18).[2] This is one of the love poems on *pālai* theme portrayed in *Kalittogai* (*KLT*), an anthology of 150 love poems. Through this love poem, the poet (through *tōḻi*) imparts the message that neither wealth nor youth nor even passionate love is permanent in this world. He emphasizes that living with his wife even in penury is much more meaningful than searching for a comfortable materialistic life leaving the wife in the home alone.

Adhering to Morality: A Virtue

In the *puṟam* poems (which are mostly addressed directly to kings/chieftains/elders/common people), poets used to convey precisely the message of morality. Guided by the principles of virtue, they don't hesitate to advise or even admonish kings at times when they intend to violate the path of virtue. For example, a poet Kōvūrkiḻār successfully thwarts the execution of two young boys (to be trampled upon by the elephants' legs) of Malaiyamāṉ who was vanquished in a battle by the Cōḻa king namely Kiḷḷivaḷavaṉ (*PNU* 46).[3]

We come across numerous poems in *puṟam* where poets convey various virtues on divergent subject matters such as God, the world, wealth, administration, duties of king/minister/officer/artisans/citizens and others. The pronouncement on virtues was very loud and clear in the body of literature produced during the post-Sangam period (*c.* 250–600 CE). Out of the "Padiṉeṉ Kīḻkkaṇakku Nūlgaḷ" (Eighteen Post-Sangam Works)—composed in a particular metre called *veṇpā*,[4] only eleven works[5] are didactic in nature while the remaining seven works[6] are non-didactic dealing with *aham* and *puṟam* themes of the Sangam literature.

The increasing influence of North over Tamiḻ land during the post-Sangam period contributed much to the development of Didactic literature in Tamiḻ. The traditional rulers of this period such as the Cēra, Cōḻa, and Pāṇḍiyas seemed to have lost their political power to intruders namely the 'Kalabhras' (of Karnataka) and consequently, there was a lot of disturbance in the peaceful life of people. In an age of internal uncertainty and near chaos, the poets showed (of course through their poems) how life should be lived and what kind of moral percepts and codes of conduct should govern it.

Tirukkuṟaḷ: The Embodiment of Ancient Tamiḻs' Ethics

Tirukkuṟaḷ (*TKḶ, c.* 250 CE), "the Universal Tamil Scripture," is composed by Tiruvaḷḷuvar in the post-Sangam period. It is the scripture—next only to the **Bible** (Christianity), the **Quran** (Islam) and the **Bhagavad Gita** (Hinduism)—widely translated into more than eighty languages. As a non-sectarian text, its all-inclusive views are indeed pioneering and very heartening. "It is a grand mosaic of cultural creation, a repertory of universal thoughts and truths. It is the one Book for all times and a world that lives by it shall enjoy eternal peace, harmony, health, wealth, power, grace and bliss" (Bharati 2008: iii). No matter is out of reach for *Tirukkuṟaḷ*. One can find each and everything—from the Godhead to ordinary entities—in it. "It gives the light of right life, the wealth of practical wisdom, the milk of heart's abundance, the honey of conjugal bliss, and the joy of peace and harmony at home and the wider homeland. It is the Gospel of 'love and give,' a code of soul-luminous (*sic.* soul-illuminating) life. The whole (of) human aspiration is epitomized in the immortal book—a book for all ages" (*Ibid*).

"The Maxims of Truth" is an eternal guiding light to humanity. It preaches ethical values, to live in moral purity, spiritual knowledge and eternal wisdom. The didactic work is a wonderful guide for any individual, be he/she a householder, homemaker, worker, artist, teacher, scholar, industrialist, politician or ruler. It consists of three sections, viz. *Aram* (Virtue), *Porul* (Wealth) and *Inbam* (Love). It clearly brings out the ideals of an enchanting family life and the excellence and beauty of ascetic life in the first section. The second section elaborates the procedures of able administration of a country. The third section deals with the delicate emotions of love. It comprises 133 chapters of ten couplets each with a total of 1,330. It has employed about 12,000 words in total, out of which less than 50 are Sanskrit. This classical ethical work employs as few words as possible, i.e., just seven words (always seven *cīr*s, seven metrical units) in every couplet to express a universal fact/truth. Not a single syllable is superfluous.

Among the eleven Didactic works of the post-Sangam period (*c.* 250–600 CE), *Tirukkural* holds the prime place for its excellent form and vivacious content comprising all kinds of virtues. It is composed in *kural veṇpā*—a two-line verse; the first line has four *cīr*s (foot) and the second line three *cīr*s. Since the whole work is scribed in *kural* metre, it bears the name *Tirukkural*. Dealing with Virtue, Wealth, and Love separately in 38, 70 and 25 *Adigāram*s (*Adhikāram* [Skt.] > *Adigāram* [Tamil], Chapters), ten couplets in each *adigāram* respectively, altogether *Tirukkural* has 1,330 *kural veṇpā*s. The concept of virtue has been explained in 380 *kural*s, whereas 700 *kural*s speak at length about the dynamics of politics, the qualities of a king as well as the subjects related to individuals. The ideal aspects of human love are aesthetically described in the last 250 *kural*s. On the whole, each *kural* dwells on a particular human quality or principle for the meaningful existence in the world.

The first *adigāram* titled "Kaḍavuḷ Vāḻttu" (Praise of God) speaks about the characteristics of the Godhead in general and about the imperative need of humanity to aspire and achieve set goals in life. Since it does not speak of any particular God, it remains uniquely non-sectarian in temper, though theistic in spirit. While defining 'Virtue' in the *adigāram* titled "Aran Valiyuruttal" (The Power of Virtue), TVR says: "Whatever is done with a spotless mind is virtue; all else is vain show" (*TKL* 44). As a firm believer in the retributive law of virtue, he cautions: "Even through forgetfulness one should not think of ruining others. If he/she does, then virtue will ruin him/her" (*TKL* 204). When people are very much concerned about gaining at least something at the cost of forsaking ethical means, Tiruvaḷḷuvar firmly rejects this view. "Whether or not one can achieve the cherished goal, the means followed to reach that goal should always be a noble one," thus he reiterates in several of his *kural*s. "Even if one sees his own mother starving, to relieve it one should not do the deeds noblemen reprove" (*TKL* 656). As a great moralist, Tiruvaḷḷuvar emphasizes that humans should lead a life of high ideals. A virtuous life sometimes may be a hindrance to the worldly life, still it is worth living. "It is better to die than lead the deceitful life of a back-biter. It will give him the benefit of what the *aram* (*Dharma* [Skt]) prescribes" (*TKL* 183).

Leading Household Life: A Greater Virtue

Giving equal importance in his work to those who lead household life and to those who lead an ascetic life, TVR emphasizes both are the ways, though different may be, to attain the goal in this birth. While speaking about the importance of domestic life and its greatness he attests: "He (householder) will be said to flourish in domestic virtue who aids the forsaken, the poor and the dead" (*TKL* 42, *Ibid.*, p. 11); "A householder who, not swerving from virtue, helps the ascetic in his way endures more than those who endure penance" (*TKL* 48, *Ibid.*). Whereas hailing the greatness of ascetic life, he pronounces, "Whatever thing, whatever thing, a man has renounced; by that thing, by that thing, (I say), he cannot suffer pain" (*TKL* 341, *Ibid.*, p. 71). "He who clings to attachment—to him do sorrows cling" (*TKL* 347). For the successful ascetic life, he prescribes several virtues to be followed in life: mercy, not killing other beings, abstinence from meat-eating, penance, steering clear of hypocrisy and fraud, truthfulness, eschewing anger, and causing suffering, evanescence of life, renunciation, realization of truth, extinction of desires and fate.

Largely influenced by Jainism, Tiruvaḷḷuvar recommends virtues aiming at dissuading the ascetic from committing social sins. For example, not to eat meat, not to resort to hypocrisy, not to cheat, not to cause injury and insult, not to destroy life—all these injunctions are aimed at weaning away the ascetic from anti-social enterprises. Once freed from such social blemishes, the ascetic could easily overcome other obstacles on the path of his spiritual journey. In a way, the recommended virtues for ascetics by TVR denote the reality of that period in which not all ascetics were free from social sins. **In the disguise of ascetic/seer/sage/hermit, nowadays we come across**

countless anti-socials that could be due to various factors such as easy accessibility to wealth, women, power and so on, but strange, it appears that in the ancient period this kind of anti-socials had also existed but with a degree of difference. That is why, it seems, TVR prescribes certain virtues to ascetics, aiming at making them perfect souls. Abstinence from killing and staying away from meat-eating, extinction of desires, hypocrisy, etc., may not observed by a householder. Whereas these virtues are obligatory and should be observed strictly by ascetics, thus pronounces TVR. "Not to kill and eat (the flesh of) an animal is better than the pouring forth of ghee in a thousand sacrifices" (*TKL* 259); "It is asked, what is the sum of all virtuous conduct? It is, never to destroy life. On the contrary, (the destruction of life) killing leads to every evil deed" (*TKL* 321). As the easy way to attain salvation, TVR emphatically pronounces: "Should anything be desired, freedom from births should be desired; that (freedom from births) will be attained by desiring to be without desire" (*TKL* 362).

Chastity: A Must Virtue for Both Men and Women

Keeping with the tradition of the Sangam age, TVR in the *adigāram* titled "Vāḻkkait Tuṇainalam" (The Virtue of a Wife), glorifies a wife by attributing several good qualities. "What is there more precious than a wife, if she possesses the stability of chastity?" (*TKL* 54); "Whatever blessing there may be, should the wife be without the virtues of the housewife, there could be no happiness" (*TKL* 52); "What is it that one lacks if one's wife is virtuous? What is it that one possesses if his wife is devoid of virtues?" (*TKL* 53). Thus, in the remaining seven *kurals* too, TVR attributes several good qualities to a wife, which are no doubt male-oriented. "They are injunctions from society, and she has to make herself worthy of praise. This chapter represents the changed climate of the age from idealized jewel of the home who had to sacrifice several strands of freedom enjoyed in the previous age. Puranic and mythical benefits are showered on her in recompense for the loss" (Manavalan 1990: 237).

In three other *adigāram*s (chapters 15, 91, 92) titled "Piraṉil Viḷaiyāmai" (Against desiring another's Wife), "Peṇvaḻic Cēṟal" (Submission to Wife Rule), and "Varaiviṉ Magaḷir" (Prostitutes) also, Tiruvaḷḷuvar speaks about women. He dissuades man from coveting another's wife in the chapter "Peṇvaḻic Cēṟal." One who desires another man's wife is castigated as a wretched and sinful being worthy of social derision. The voice of Tiruvaḷḷuvar is: "Hatred, sin, fear and disgrace— these four will never leave him who goes into his neighbour's wife" (*TKḶ* 146); "The folly of desiring her, who is the property of another will not be found in those who know (the attributes of) virtue and (the rights of) property" (*TKḶ* 141).

While the chapter "Vāḻkkait Tuṇainalam" exhorts the wife to guard her chastity as her primary duty, the chapter "Piraṉil Viḷaiyāmai" urges the man not to desire another man's wife. In both instances, the wife is treated as lifelong property—neither is she permitted to step beyond her threshold, nor is anyone else allowed to transgress the boundaries of this proprietary claim. Manavalan opines: "The situation gradually changed and before or around the dawn of the Christian Era, the concept of personal property as a social system came into being and the warrior class, merchant class and the disintegrated chieftains of Vēḷir class became the owner of the property. As with the kings for territory, these newly propertied classes might have started violating the social laws by force of might. Such a 'might is right' situation needed some checks. The period of 'Didactic Literature,' i.e., from the *c.* A.D. 200 to 600 might have witnessed such effort at stabilization of social rights" (*Ibid.*, pp. 237–38).

In the same vein of exhorting the women to protect their chastity, Tiruvaḷḷuvar censures men against visiting prostitutes. In the chapter "Varaiviṉ Magaḷir," he severely condemns the menfolk who visit prostitutes. He asserts: "Those whose knowledge is made excellent by their (natural) sense will not covet the trifling delights of those whose favours are common (to all)" (*TKḺ* 915, trs. Drew and John Lazarus 1983: 185). Subsequently, *TVR seems to be 'the first Tamiḻ poet-moralist' to emphasize male chastity.*

Boozing, Gambling and Begging: Evil Deeds

In a similar tone, Tiruvaḷḷuvar condemns other social evils such as drinking toddy/liquor, gambling, begging, etc., as well. Drinking *kaḷ* (toddy) was a common food culture among the people of the Sangam period. Nowhere in the entire body of Sangam corpus, drinking is condemned as evil. Whereas TVR highlights the evils of drinking. "Let no liquor be drunk; it is desired, let it be drunk by those who care not for esteem of the great" (*TKḺ* 922); "They that sleep resemble the dead; they that drunk are no other than poison-eaters" (*TKḺ* 926). Thus, he reasons against the drinking of liquor.

As a great moralist, perhaps aware of the consequences of gambling portrayed in the epic *Mahābhārata*, TVR severely criticizes gambling as a serious social evil as follows: "Never indulge in gambling, profitable though it may be. Gambling gains spell danger like the angler's bait to the fish" (*TKḺ* 931). "There is nothing else that brings poverty like gambling which causes many a misery and destroys (one's) reputation" (*TKḺ* 934, *Ibid.*, p. 189).

Ethically, TVR seems to be critical of the preceding 'Heroic Age' (*c.* 3000 BCE–300 CE), where imploring for food and fortune by the learned and the needy was an unpleasant part of human life. Considering begging as a wretched social disease, he serves the dictum that one should not beg even if it affords him 'heaven.' "There is nothing more disgraceful to one's tongue than to use it in begging for a drought of water even for a cow" (*TKḺ* 1066, *Ibid.*, p. 215), thus he shows his concern. Worried much for the people who live in utter poverty, he declares: "If the Creator of the world has decreed even begging as means of livelihood, may he too go a begging and perish" (*TKḺ* 1062, *Ibid.*). But in an altogether different point of view—contrary to discouraging begging TVR glorifies: "Whatsoever is spoken in the world will abide as praise upon that man who gives alms to the poor" (*TKḺ* 232, *Ibid.*, p. 49); "To beg is evil, even though it were said that is a good path (to heaven). To give is good even though it were said that those who do so cannot obtain heaven" (*TKḺ* 222, *Ibid.*, p. 47). Thus, on the one hand, he severely discourages begging, on the other hand, he sincerely encourages giving alms to the poor, against any odds. Not in a position to alleviate the misery of the jobless poor other than appealing to the rich to help them, TVR seems to be suggesting a humanitarian viewpoint: the *haves* should support the *have-nots*, in their own interest of not causing a potential revolution against their own lot.

Being a poet-moralist, who lived during the heyday of monarchical rule, Tiruvaḷḷuvar prescribes various virtues to be observed in politics too, which are relevant even today.

In the chapter (55) "Ceṅkōṉmai" (On the Rule of the Right Sceptre), he points out: "The world will constantly embrace the feet of the monarch who rules his subjects with love" (*TKL* 544). Again, to a monarch, he asserts: "It is not the spear but the unbending sceptre (or rule of law) that will yield victory" (*TKL* 546). "A ruler who extracts money from his subjects unjustly is no better than a highway-robber holding a lance and dispossessing the victims of their wealth" (*TKL* 552). "The tears of grief shed by the oppressed subjects are a strong weapon which will wipe off a monarch's wealth" (*TKL* 555). Thus, **what all he pronounced as royal codes for the kings/ monarchs of his days, that all could even now be applicable to the democratic rulers.** Despite far-reaching changes in the material life of the people due to scientific discoveries in the preceding and present centuries, transcending all limitations, **baring a few ideas, almost all Tiruvaḷḷuvar's thoughts on individuals and the state are aptly applicable to the present-day world.** It is indeed a herculean task to discuss all the virtues emphasized by TVR in his ethical treatise, which remains one the finest archetypal literary expressions of the didactic genre in Tamiḻ.

Major Virtues Illustrated in Nāladiyār

Next to *Tirukkuṟaḷ*, a universally acclaimed didactic work, the second best known Tamiḻ work in this genre, is *Nāladiyār* (*NDR*), a composition of 400 quatrains in *veṇpā* metre. It is a joint literary work of a group of Jaina authors, collected and classified by Padumaṉār whose date is unknown. The tone of the work is strongly ascetic and cynical. It emphasizes almost all the virtues advocated in the *TKL* but in a different manner. The *NDR*, exactly like *TKL*, has three divisions or sections titled "Aṟattuppāl" (Section on Virtue), "Poruṭpal" (Section on Wealth) and "Iṉbattuppāl" ("Section on Love") and each section comprises several chapters. True to Jaina philosophy, the *NDR* contains several quatrains that emphasize virtuous living, favouring a life of renunciation domesticity. Many verses highlight the transient nature of worldly existence, including the impermanence of the body, wealth, and other material aspects. "Even the rich people, who had selected the best of delicacies served by their wives might go begging for gruel at times. Therefore, never think that wealth is a permanent one" (*NDR* 1), thus it warns about the impermanence of wealth. About the transient nature of the body, it pronounces: "The orchard loses its glamour once the fruit-gathering season is over. Likewise, youth loses all its elegance over time. Do not be taken up by her sharp spear-shaped bewitching eyes. Her alluring beauty and youth will give way to old age. Bent down with age and indifferent sight, she will guide herself with a stick" (*NDR* 17). "Speech falters, they lean on a staff, and walk tottering, these teeth fall out; yet till the vessel (body) is scorned by all they linger in the house, still indulging in fond desires; to these, no way of safety opens out" (*NDR* 13).

These verses clearly indicate the change of worldview (from the point of Jaina monks) from *TKL* which prefers domestic life to the other. Both *Tirukkuṟaḷ* and *Nālaḍiyār* agree to a greater extent on personal virtues. While the former treats the theme of the transient nature of the world in one chapter, the latter elaborates on it in three separate chapters describing the evanescence of youth, the body and worldly pleasures. In keeping with its emphasis on "life-negation," the *NDR* discredits the beauty and charm of women and even praising the virtue of chastity, it accords rather less glory to women than *TKḶ*. Its emphasis on education is more eloquent and elaborate than that of *TKḶ* in some respects.

> Learning knows no bounds: The learner's days are few.
> Think of it with calm: There's a lot of maladies.
> Learn with clear discrimination what there is to learn,
> Like the heron which leaves water and drinks milk.

> (*Nālaḍiyār*, 135, tr. Kamil Zvelebil 1974: 124)

Being an anthology of verses composed by several unknown versifiers, there are some verses that contradict themselves in certain maxims such as nobility of birth, concept attributing high or low to a person and so on. According to Jaina philosophy, an individual encounters fortune or misfortune, and develpos good or bad character, in accordance with the laws of *Karma*. *Karma* means something done, whether as cause or effect. Actions in harmony with *dharma* bring *good karma* and add to health and happiness. Selfish actions, at odds with the rest of life, bring *unfavourable karma* and pain, according to the *Karma* theory. Just as one cannot swim against the current of a wild river, one cannot defy what is predestined. In contrast, the *Tirukkuṟaḷ* says that the destiny can be overcome through ceaseless, conscious effort or by associating with the great and the wise men. Although the text draws on several ideas from Jainism, it affirms only the theory of association. For example, on the matter of death, it observes: "To them that have attained the power of penance, it is possible even to leap over death" (*TKḶ* 269). Whereas *NḌR* affirms: "Man's days pass not their assigned bound. None here on earth have ever escaped death's power, made off and got free" (*NḌR* 6, tr. Pope).[7] When *TKḶ* insists on man's efforts and environment, the *NḌR* favours the fruits of one's *karma*.

A Few Virtues Illustrated in Other Tamiḻ Didactic Works

The remaining nine works of "Padiṉeṉ Kīḻkkaṇakku Nūlgaḷ" (Post-Eighteen Literary Works) are less popular as didactic works in Tamiḻ. Each by an individual poet, these works of a lesser repute more or less repeat the same virtues as described in *TKḶ* and *NDR*. Not structured into chapters, these compositions do not have verses of similar ideas grouped together. Each poem is to be read to understand the subject of teaching. At times there are repetitions, and often and again, the same virtue is described differently. Among these didactic works, *Paḻamoḻi Nāṉūṟu, Nāṉmaṇikkaḍigai* have some effects on Tamiḻs. *Paḻamoḻi Nāṉūṟu*, similar to *NDR* in terms of form and content, is a collection of 400 quatrains by a Jain author called Muṉṟuṟai Araiyaṉār. Each verse concludes with a proverb that encapsulates the idea conveyed in the preceding three lines. The aesthetic appeal lies in the aptness of the proverb—not only in its use of vivid idioms but also in its ability to effectively reinforce and complete the argument for the reader. For example, the versifier wants to advise people against retaliation or revenge by using a popular proverb. "If worthless people prefer to do some harm, great people will not return the harm even as no man bites the dog in retaliation of its angry bite" (*Paḻamoḻi Nāṉūṟu* 49). Thus, the verse conveys the message effectively to the readers. "As proverbs are more or less proven facts of social reality transmitted through generation by generation, their use as an illustration of the ideas conveyed readily convinces the reader. The author of this work makes use of this device for a better heuristic function" (Manavalan, *Op. cit.*, p. 243).

The other didactic composition *Nāṉmaṇikkaḍigai* is a short work of 103 verses of *veṇpā* metre authored by Viḷambi Nāgaṉār. The title means "the Salver of Four Gems" and stands to signify that each of its verses contains four statements or aspects of virtue that are somehow associated with each other through antithesis, comparison, or illustration. "In terms of poetic function, it is superior to *Palamoli Nānūru* and many of its statements have passed into the folklore of the Tamils" (*Ibid.*).

The other remaining didactic works such as *Tirikaḍugam, Cirupañcamūlam, Ēlādi, Innā Nārpadu* and *Iniyavai Nārpadu* are modelled on *Nānmaṇikkaḍigai.* Of these, the first three are named after the number of medicinal ingredients suggested by the name. The *Tirikaḍugam* by Nallādanār means "Composed of Three Spices," namely dry ginger, long pepper and black pepper. Each of the 100 verses makes three statements in the form of instruction.

> Acquire wealth in order to give;
> Learn great works that you may walk in the way of virtue;
> Speak every word with gracious purpose;
> These are the paths that conduct not to the world of darkness.
>
> (*Tirikaḍugam* 90, tr. Pope)[8]

Cirupañcamūlam, a composition of 100 verses, means "Concoction of Five Herbs." Each verse contains five statements. *Ēlādi*, meaning "Compounded Six Medicinal Things," as such contains five or six virtues in each verse. "The idea behind such titles is that just as these ingredients help maintain the body in good health, the virtues described in these works help man develop and maintain a healthy and ethical behaviour in life" (Manavalan, *Op. cit.*, p. 244). It emphatically lists out some of the virtues that could lead a man to a meaningful life.

> Good it is, not killing; evil it is killing.
> Bad it is, not learning; harmful it is angry.
> Good it is, not slandering a person before others.
>
> (*Cirupañcamūlam* 51, tr. Author)

Innā Nārpadu and *Iniyavai Nārpadu* are two companion verses of 40 stanzas each, making statements about the desirables and undesirables in life. As such, they offer profound observations on life, many of which are expressed through striking idioms. Let us take note of the statements made in *Innā Nārpadu* and *Iniyavai Nārpadu* on the desirable and undesirable things:

> Difficult it is leading a conjugal life
> with the non-compatible wife;
> Harmful it is having friendship with
> narrow minded (low class) people;
> Harmful it is having relationship with womanizers;
> Distress it is seeing a creditor getting into the house.
>
> (*Innā Nārpadu* 12, tr. Author)
>
> Pleasant it is to have the honour of
> not desiring another's wife;
> Good it is the withering crops having the rain;
> Pleasant it is the brave king hearing the rut elephant's
> roaring at his backyard
>
> (*Iniyavai Nārpadu* 16, tr. Author)

Ācārakkōvai (*ĀK*) containing 100 *veṇpā*s of unequal length is more spiritual in aim and much ritualistic in tone. Meaning "the Garland of Right Conduct," its main concern is to teach good manners and virtuous conduct to man in life both at home and in society. It is not only a collection of moral exhortations but also of ritual observations and customs considered proper and correct. As such, it prescribes daily routine and religious practices to be followed in life. For example: "Those who care for proper manners do not eat before providing it to guests, elders, cows, slaves and children" (*ĀK* 21).[9]

Mudumoḻikkāñci, another didactic work of this group, consists of 100 lines in all, divided into ten equal sections. In each line of four feet, an ethical instruction is imparted with internal rhyme and alliteration, facilitating easy memorization. The tone of instruction can be heard in the following lines. "Not a wife she is, who is not leading a life according to the nature of the husband; not life it is, which is not honoured by the wife" (*Mudumoḻikkāñci*, "Alla Pattu" 1 & 2).

The lesser-known didactic works discussed above generally reveal a gradual change of worldview, change of emphasis on certain virtues and inclusion of several new virtues to accommodate the slowly changing phase of the then-contemporary society. Baring a few, all the didactic works deal with virtues such as good birth, domestic life, learning, almsgiving/ hospitality, association of good people, abstaining from drinking alcohol and meat-eating and upright government.

"Thematically speaking, the heyday of Tamiḻ didactic literature remains to be the period of the great *Kīḻkkaṇakku* works. They had a far greater vision of human merits and demerits: the role of human beings on earth, the true meaning of human life and the essentials and non-essentials of our earthly life. Though there seems to have been tension between a poetic pull and the worldviews, life-affirmation and life-negation, their relative merits were never forgotten and their complementary nature never lost sight of. Though some minor works have leaned at times this way or that way, great works like *Kuṟaḷ, Nālaṭiyār, Nānmaṇikkaṭigai,* and *Nītineṟi Viḷakkam* did not succumb to these philosophical pulls but steered ahead with their eyes fixed on the common human nature and nurture. And hence their emphasis is on life rather than on the particular and consequently their conditioned relevance even to modern times" (Manavalan, *Ibid.*, pp. 250–51).

The eighteen Didactic works are not only known for their themes, but they are also known for their peculiar verse form, metre called *veṇpā*. When poets like Tiruvaḷḷuvar desired to convey the message of virtues to mankind, for that they have carefully chosen this particular metre, which is eminently suitable to gnomic poetry. The *veṇpā* is the most difficult and most highly esteemed stanza structure of classical Tamiḻ literature. There are five kinds of *veṇpā* stanzas.[10] Tiruvaḷḷuvar just skilfully employs a kind of *veṇpā* known as *Kuṟaḷ Veṇpā* (the shortest *veṇpā*) in his *magnum opus*.

The structural properties of *veṇpā* are as follows:

(a) Only feet of three or two metrical units may be employed.

(b) The stanza must always end in a foot of the following type: *nāḷ, malar, kāsu, piṟappu.*[11]

(c) Strict rules of consonance of lines must be observed (so called *veṇ toḍai*).

(d) The numbers of lines are two in the case of *kuṟaḷ veṇpā*; three in the case of *cindiyal veṇpā*; four in the cases of *nērisai veṇpā* and *iṉṉisai veṇpā*; form five to twelve lines in the case of *pahṟoḍai veṇpā*.

(e) The last line consists of three feet only. The remaining line(s) each consist(s) of four feet.

As an instance, let us see the structural properties of *kuṟaḷ veṇpā* (393) as analyzed by Kamil Zvelebil in his brilliant research book titled *Smile of Murugan* (1973: 166–67) to understand them properly.

> *kaṇṇuḍaiya reṉbavar kaṟṟār mugattiraṇḍu*
> *puṇṇuḍaiyar kallā davar*   (TKḺ 393)
>
> The learned men alone are said to have eyes:
> The unlearned have but a pair of sores in their face.
>
> Its metric structure is:

nāḷ+malar+nāḷ / nāḷ+malar / nāḷ+nāḷ / malar+malar+nāḷ
nāḷ+malar+nāḷ / nāḷ+nāḷ / malar.

Observe how the aforementioned rules are strictly followed: the couplet consists of four feet in the first line and three in the second, with each foot comprising only two or three metrical units. The couplet concludes with a foot of the type known as *malar*. Note also the close and intricate connection between the formal structure and the content. It is precisely this perfect form—beyond its metrical precision and structural meaning—that lends beauty and force to what might otherwise appear as rather banal 'sayings,' imbuing the couplets with their undeniable poetic power in the original (Zvelebil 1973: 167).

When poets composed the verses of didactic spirit meant for social righteousness by making individuals morally perfect, they intently chose the small form of a poetical metre. Since all these verses have to be recited or quoted—again and again whenever necessary even in our modern times—only through memory, it was quite natural and just handy for the poets to use this particular *veṇpā* metre, which proved them right even after nearly two millennia.

Notes

*	This essay is the slightly revised version of my article titled "Didactic Literature in Tamiḻ: A Genre for Social Cause," published in *Major Genres and Trends in Dravidian Literature (Classical)*, Prof. R. Sri Hari (General Editor), Dravidian University, Kuppam–517425, 2003, pp. 151–64.

1.	Source: http://www.merriam-webster.com/dictionary/didactic

2.   *arumporuḷ vēṭkaiyiṉ uḷḷam turappap*
     pirinduṟai cūḻādi aiya virumbinī
     eṉtōḷ eḻudiya toyyilum yāḻaniṉ
     mainduḍai mārbil cuṇangum niṉaittukkāṇ
     ceṉṟōr mugappap poruḷum kiḍavādu
     oḻindavar ellārum uṇṇādum cellār
     iḷamaiyum kāmamum ōrāngup peṟṟār
     vaḷamai viḻaitakkadu uṇḍō uḷanāḷ
     orōogai tammuḷ taḻīi orōogai
     oṉṟaṉ kūṟāḍai uḍuppavarē āyiṉum
     oṉṟiṉār vāḻkkaiyē vāḻkkai aridarō
     ceṉṟa iḷamai taraṟku!

     (*Kalittogai* 18)

     Lord, do not consider leaving, goaded by your
     mind, and thirsting for precious wealth!
     Think about the thoyyil designs that you painted
     on my arms lovingly, and the pallor spots I got
     embracing your mighty chest.

     Wealth does not lie around for those who go in
     search of it. Also, those who do not leave to earn
     wealth do not starve.

     Will those with youth and love for each other
     desire to seek material wealth? Living life is living
     with love, embracing each other with one hand and
     covering torn clothes with the other hand.
     It is not possible to bring back youth that would be lost!

     (*Kalittogai* 18, Pālai Pāḍiya Peruṅkaḍuṅkō, tr. Vaidehi Herbert)

     Source: https://sangamtranslationsbyvaidehi.com/ettuthokai kalithokai-
             palai-1-36/

3.   *nīyē puṟaviṉ allalaṉṟiyum piṟavum*
     iḍukkaṇ palavum viḍuttōṉ maruganai
     ivarē pulaṉuḻu duṇmārpuṉkaṉ añcit
     tamaḍupagut tuṇṇum taṉṉilal vāḻnar
     kaḷiṟukaṇ ḍaḻūum aḻāal maṟanda

puntalaic ciṟāar maṉṟumaruṇḍu nōkki
virundiṟ puṉkaṉō vuḍaiyar
kēṭṭaṉai yāyiṉī vēṭṭadu ceymmē.

(Kōvūrkiḻār to Kiḷḷivaḷavaṉ, *Puṟanāṉūṟu* 46)

You come from the line of Cōḻa king
who gave his flesh
for a pigeon in danger,
        and for others besides,

and these children also come
from a line of kings
who in their cool shade
share all they have

lest poets,
those tillers of nothing
but wisdom,
should suffer hardships.

> Look at these children,
> the crowns of their heads are still soft.
> As they watch the elephants,
> they even forget to cry,
>
> stare dumbstruck at the crowd
> in some new terror
> of things unknown.

Now that you've heard me out,
do what you will.

(Kōvūrkiḻār to Kiḷḷivaḷavaṉ, *Puṟanāṉūṟu* 46,
tr. Ramanujan 1985: 122)

4. *Veṇpā* literally means "the white metre of prosody" (*veṇ* = white,
    pā = metre of prosody). Perhaps it might be 'the serene metre' of
    Tamiḻ prosody. It is one of the four metres of ancient Tamiḻ prosody.
    The other three metres of ancient Tamiḻ prosody are: *āciriyappā*,
    vañcippā and *kalippā*. Its *ōsai* (the rhythmic sound) is *ceppal* (telling
    or discoursing mode). As a form of classical Tamiḻ poetry, *veṇpā*
    consists of between two and twelve lines.

Vowels and consonant–vowel compounds in Tamiḻ alphabet have been classified into ones with short sounds (*kuṟil*) and the ones with long sounds (*neḍil*). A sequence of one or more of these units optionally followed by a consonant can form a *nēr asai* (the Tamiḻ word *asai* roughly corresponds to a syllable in English) or a *nirai asai* depending on the duration of pronunciation. *Nēr* and *nirai* are the basic units of meter in Tamiḻ prosody. A *cīr* is a type of metrical foot that roughly corresponds to an iamb in English. *Taḷai* is the juxtaposition of iambic patterns.

Note that the official terms for the different *asai*s are self-descriptive. For example, the word *nēr* is itself classified as *nēr asai*. And the word *nirai* is a *nirai asai*.

A set of well-defined metric rules define the grammar for *veṇpā*. One set of rules constrains the duration of sound for each word or *cīr*, while another set of rules defines the rules for the possible sounds at the beginning of a word that follows a given sound at the end of the preceding word. Any *venpa* should conform to both these sets of rules.

Following is the set of production rules corresponding to the first set of rules.

Veṇpā	→	<aḍi> {1-11} <īrraḍi>
Aḍi	→	<cīr> <cīr> <cīr> <cīr>
Īrraḍi	→	<cīr> <cīr> <īrruccīr>
Cīr	→	<īrrasai> | <mūvasai>
Īrruccīr	→	<nāḷ> | <malar> | <kāsu> | <piṟappu>
Īrrasai	→	<tēmā> | <pulimā> | <karuviḷam> | <kūviḷam>
Muvasai	→	<tēmāṅkāy> | <pulimāṅkāy> | <karuviḷaṅkāy> | <kūviḷaṅkāy>
Tēmā	→	<nēr> <nēr>
Pulimā	→	<nirai> <nēr>
Karuviḷam	→	<nirai> <nirai>
Kūviḷam	→	<nēr> <nirai>
Tēmāṅkāy	→	<nēr> <nēr> <nēr>
Pulimāṅkāy	→	<nirai> <nēr> <nēr>
Karuviḷaṅkāy	→	<nirai> <nirai> <nēr>
Kūviḷaṅkāy	→	<nēr> <nirai> <nēr>
Nāḷ	→	<nēr+consonant>
Malar	→	<nirai+consonant>

Kāsu	→	<*nēr* +*nēr*>
Pirappu	→	<*nirai*+consonant+*nirai*>
Nēr	→	<*kuril*> or <*neḍil*> | *kuril/neḍil*> + <consonant>
Nirai	→	< 2 *kurils*> or <*kuril*+*neḍil*> | <2 *kurils*+consonant or *kuril*+*neḍil*+consonant>
Kuril	=	short vowel (*a, i, u, e, o*)
Neḍil	=	long vowel (*ā, ī, ū, ē, ō*) and diphthongs (*ai, au*)

5. Eleven Didactic Works: 1. *Tirukkuraḷ*, 2. *Nāladiyār*, 3. *Palamoli Nānūru*, 4. *Nānmaṇikkaḍigai*, 5. *Tirikaḍugam*, 6. *Cirupañcamūlam*, 7. *Ācārakkōvai*, 8. *Ēlādi*, 9. *Innā Nārpadu*, 10, *Iniyavai Nārpadu*, 11. *Mudumoḷikkāñci*.

6. Seven Non-Didactic Works: 1. *Kār Nārpadu*, 2. *Kaḷavaḷi Nārpadu*, 3. *Tiṇaimoḷi Aimpadu*, 4. *Aintiṇai Aimpadu*, 5. *Aintiṇai Eḷupadu*, 6. *Tiṇaimālai Nūrraimpadu*, 7. *Kainnilai*.

7. *Nāladiyār* verse 6, tr. Pope, Quoted in *Encyclopaedia of Tamiḷ Literature*, Vol. I, Dr. Shu Hikosaka, Institute of Asian Studies, Chennai, 1990, p. 243.

8. *Tirikaḍugam* 90, tr. Pope, *Ibid.*, p. 244.

9. For more details, please see the third chapter titled "From Sleeping to Salvation: Vedic Codes and Practices."

10. Five kinds of *Veṇpā*: 1) *Kuraḷ Veṇpā*, 2) *Nērisai Veṇpā*, 3) *Innisai Veṇpā*, 4) *Cindiyal Veṇpā*, 5) *Pahroḍai* (*Paltoḍai*) *Veṇpā*.

11. *Nāḷ*: (*nēr asai*) – a foot consists of a short vowel or a long vowel + a consonant).

    Malar: (*nirai asai*) – a foot consists of a pair of short vowels with or without a consonant).

    Kāsu: (*nērbu asai*) – a foot consists of a short or long vowel with or without a consonant + a short vowel consonant ending with '*u.*'

    Pirappu: (*niraibu asai*) – a foot consists of a pair of short vowels with or without a consonant + a short vowel consonant ending with '*u.*'

Chapter – Two

Familiar Terms and Unfamiliar Connotations: Cultural Undertones in Tirukkuṟaḷ*

Every language has two categories—'spoken language' and 'written language.' No language functions without 'sounds,' otherwise known as 'phonemes,' 'words'/'terms' and 'sentences.' A 'term' could be merely a sound or a syllable, or a unit of sounds or syllables. Almost all terms denote something or the other. Some terms may *signify* a grammatical tradition, while others *signify* the cultural aspects of a given language within its historical evolution. Furthermore, some terms may even denote the culture of an ethnicity, either explicitly or implicitly. Some unique terms–such as *cāṉṟōṉ* (a noble man), *nōkku* (the sight of love), *naṭpu* (love, i.e., the sexual relationship), *virundu* (novelty), *naṉṟi* (a good deed), and *nāṟṟam* (fragrance), as rendered in the classical Sangam works and post-Sangam works like *Tirukkuṟaḷ*–have acquired different connotations in the Tamil texts, spanning a period over 2000 years. These terms effectively reflect the socio-political, religious, and cultural life of Tamils of the preceding eras. As such, they *signify* the cultural mobility of Tamils, an ethnicity of the 'Heroic Age' (*c.* 3000 BCE–300 CE). For instance, a unique term *cāṉṟōr* which specifically meant "warriors" in the Sangam age, however, referred to "noble men"/"men of virtue" in the Didactic period (*c.*

250–600 CE), "courageous men" or "men of justice" in the *Ci-lappadigāram* (*c.* 300 CE), "slaves of the lord" (*Nāyaṉmārs* and *Āḻvārs*) during the Bhakti Movement (*c.* 600–900 CE), "prodigious Sangam poets" in the *Kamba Rāmāyaṇam* (*c.* 1200 CE), and "distinguished"/"dignified men of holding some eminent and prominent position" in the present Tamiḻ society. Apparently, several reasons contributed to the evolution of numerous meanings of the terms mentioned above. In the quest for understanding the cultural dynamics of the Tamiḻs, the present essay aims at divulging the cultural undertones of the aforesaid terms in *Tirukkuṟaḷ* in detail.

Culture – Cultural Mobility

Man is a social being. The manner/conduct/behaviour of one's 'inner-self' (heart) may be termed as "culture." The actions of man's 'outer-self' (body/physique) may be known as "civilization." No one's/no ethnicity's culture and civilization remain intact forever. They change/transform according to the demands of situations. A person who acts in a certain manner at a particular time will have changes in her/his conduct of the inner and outer-selves. The socio-political-economic, and religious conditions of a given period significantly influence an individual's or a community's culture and civilization. The shifts and transformations that affect both the inner and outer dimensions of a person or an ethnicity may be referred to as "cultural mobility."

Tirukkuṟaḷ: Age and Matters

As stated in the previous chapter, the *Tirukkuṟaḷ* composed by Tiruvaḷḷuvar during the post-Sangam period, stands as the only work in Tamiḻ literature often referred to as "the Maxims of Truth." It comprehensively addresses a wide spectrum of virtues and lofty ideals relevant to all of humanity. In addition to imparting essential political knowledge and ethical codes and conducts for both rulers and citizens, this "universally acclaimed didactic treatise" also explores, with aesthetic sensitivity, the nuanced human emotion known as "love." (For more details, please see passages under the heading "Tirukkuṟaḷ: The Embodiment of Ancient Tamiḻs' Ethics" in the previous chapter).

Evidently, at the hind of the 'Heroic Age,' the life of valour has seen losing its sheen. This was the age in which the kings ruled their countries despotically with enormous powers. Jainism and Buddhism had a hold on people by propagating the ideals of "world negation" and upholding the life of "renunciation." People then started to deviate from the tenets of compassion-dignity-discipline. They were bound by evil practices such as lying, stealing, passion, greed, anger, cunning, lust for other's wives, etc. Also, they became addicted to evil habits such as boozing (drinking toddy/liquor) and gambling. Much obsessed with accumulating wealth, people started deviating from the path of righteousness, honesty and probity. The Tamiḻ society of the bygone era was moving away from its cherished principles for the first time in history. In this degenerated scenario, there emerged the ever great ethical treatise *Tirukkuṟaḷ*. It has emphasized the need for upholding the life of virtue/righteousness in inner and outer spheres at individual-familial-and societal levels. So, "the Great Maxim" has often employed a unique term *cāṉṟōṉ* at several places so as to emphasize the great dividends one can reap by leading a virtuous life.

I

Cāṉṟōṉ: Learned/Noble Man

Cāṉṟōṉ is a unique literary term in Tamiḻ that has been occurring time and again with different connotations, right from Sangam poems to contemporary Tamiḻ literature. It is a noun exclusively referring to the masculine gender singular (plural. *cāṉṟōr/ cāṉṟavar*). The term generally denotes *ariñaṉ* (a scholar), *kaṟṟōṉ*, (a learned), *periyōṉ*, (a great man) (Kathiraiverpillai 1984: 620), *naṟpaṇbu niṟaindavaṉ*, (a man of noble qualities) (Varadara-janar 1974: 14). The actual meaning of the term *cāṉṟōṉ/cāṉṟōr* is *cāṉṟāṇmai* (sublimity/virtue/goodness),[1] the men of *cālbuk-kuṇaṅgaḷ*[2] (the attributes of perfection, viz. love, modesty, beneficence, benignant grace and truth), (Pope 2009: 200); *māṭciyiṟ periyōr*[3] (the great personae of glorious traits). *Cāṉṟōṉ*, 'the esteemed person' is highly respected by everybody as 'a great man,' mostly because of his high knowledge and fine character. The term strikingly refers to *an exceptional warrior, a great man, a noble man* and *excellent poets of the Sangam period* (Vaiyapurip-pillai 1982: 1397). It suffices to say that the *cāṉṟōr* (singular *cāṉṟōṉ*) are the people known for excellent characteristics. The notions of the excellent characteristics or attributes of great persons change from time to time as befitting the prevailing significant culture of the Tamiḻs. The excellent attribute was *valour/prowess* (*vīram* in Tamiḻ) in the Sangam Age. Nonetheless, the same term meant differently to denote *the erudite scholarship-wisdom-righteousness* in the post-Sangam period; *impeccable quality of justice* in *Cilappadigāram*; *holiness/divinity* during the Bhakti Movement heydays; *extraordinary poetic skill of Sangam works* in the *Kamba Rāmāyaṇam*, and *the dignity/eminence and prominence/scholarship in Tamiḻ* in the present Tamiḻ society.

Cāṉrōṉ in Sangam Works (*c.* 200 BCE–200 CE): Warrior/Noble Man

The ancient Tamiḻ society consisted of several clans virtually shaped into many kingdoms and empires during the Sangam age. The kings of the ancient period have shown utmost interest in expanding their kingdoms rather than protecting their own territories. Countless battles/wars were waged time and again. Hence, there arose a great need for warriors—physically strong and mentally shrewd to protect their land. In fact, 'the great warriors,' emerging triumphant from battles/wars, were highly respected and regarded. They were suitably felicitated with lavish gifts/awards/honours. Against this backdrop, a woman poet named Poṉmuḍiyār, upon embracing household life, enlists her societal duty and that of others in the following poem from *Puraṉāṉūru* (*PNU*) anthology.[4] She pronounces:

> To bring forth and rear a son is my (foremost) duty.
> To make him noble (warrior) is the father's.
> To make spears for him is the blacksmith's.
> To show him good ways is the king's.
>
> And to bear
> a bright sword and do battle,
> to butcher enemy elephants, and come back:
>
> that is the young man's duty.
>
> (*PNU* 312, tr. Ramanujan 1985: 185)
>
> (The words in parenthesis are added by the author)

This poem echoes the ancient predominant patriarchal point of view. The poetess Poṉmuḍiyār apparently declares that bringing forth and rearing a son is her foremost duty. Her husband's (the father of her son) duty is to bring up the child as *cāṉrōṉ*, 'the warrior' (not 'wise' or 'noble (man)' as translated by Kamil Zvelebil, A.K. Ramanujan, and George L Hart respectively cited earlier); blacksmith's to make spears for him; the king's to offer him a fitting job in his army; finally the duty of the *kāḷai* (ox/bull which denotes here *a valiant youth*) is to come back home victorious after fighting indomitably with his shining sword, after killing wild elephants on battlefield. In the interest of apprehending the exact or contextual meaning of the term *cānrōn*, we should take the term *kāḷai* (appearing in the last stanza) into consideration for proper understanding. The term *kāḷai* in Tamil refers to 'a young bull' or 'ox.' Here the term is rendered as a *signifier* for signifying 'the chivalrous warrior.' If we consider the other interpretations such as "a wise (man)" (Zvelebil 1974: 47), "a noble (man)" (Ramanujan 1985: 185), "a noble man" (Hart 1999: 180) as rendered to the aforesaid term by the eminent translators, then the actual motif of the poem will be paradoxical. Why because the protagonist of the poem is undoubtedly *a chivalrous warrior*. Only to *a valiant hero*, a blacksmith is expected to make spears, the king is supposed to offer him a suitable position in his army, and finally, who returns triumphantly from the battlefield after eliminating the wild elephants, can only be called a *kāḷai*, a youthful bull.

Any woman naturally should have numerous duties to perform in her familial life. But conspicuously, rearing a warrior/gallant/valiant/chivalrous son seems to be *the foremost duty* of the women of Sangam period.' During that period, a father was expected to facilitate his son to become *a warrior youth but not a wise or noble man*. The duties of the blacksmith, king and finally the youth enlisted in the poem did contextually corroborate the fact of making a youth, a warrior. This can be testified and substantiated by another poem, appearing from the same *Puranānūru* anthology,[5] penned by a poetess named Kāvarpeṇḍu. A young girl, out of some interest in a young man, enquires from his mother about her son's whereabouts. Then his mother replies with great pride:

> You stand against the pillar
> of my hut and ask:
> > Where is your son?
>
> I don't really know.
> This womb was once
> a lair
> for that tiger.
>
> You can see him now
> only on battlefields.

(Kāvarpeṇḍu, *Puranāṇūṟu* 86, tr. Ramanujan 1985: 184)

It is quite evident from the Tamiḻ poem as well as from its English rendering that one can understand the proud sentiment of the mothers who were hugely delighted at the heroic/gallant/ valiant personality of their sons. The mothers, as shown in the Sangam poems, indeed, feel proud of rearing heroic sons.

The "mother sentiment" does not show any affection or lenience to cowardly sons, even by a whisper. An old woman in *Puranāṇūṟu* hears a rumour that her son has died showing his back on the battlefield. She instantly becomes enraged and thunders: "If does he show his back and run away from the ferocious battle, I will cut off these breasts that fed him" (*maṇḍamark kuḍaindaṉa ṉāyiṉ uṇḍaveṉ/ mulaiyaṟut tiḍuvēṉ yāṉ*). She turns over everybody lying on the blood-soaked battlefield. She finally finds her son who was chopped to pieces and feels happier than the day she had borne him! (Kākkaipāḍiṉiyār Naccellaiyār, *PNU* 278). This is the predominant sense attached to the men of bravery and heroism. It is in this sense, the king as the patron of warriors is denoted in the stanza, *cāṉṟōr puravala* (the patron of warriors) in *Padiṟṟuppattu* (55: 1) as well.

Contrary to this specific connotation, the term *cāṉṟōr* is rarely rendered to denote in general *noble men* in some poems (e.g., *PNU* 191).[6] When heroic excellence was the most adored merit among the characteristics of youths of Sangam age, however, Zvelebil (1973: 17) interprets the term *cāṉṟōṉ* differently another way. While elaborating the meaning of the Tamil term *cāṉṟōr,* he observes: "This (*cāṉṟōṉ*) is a participle noun derived from the verb stem *cāl,* "to be abundant, full, suitable, filling, great, noble," the noun *cāl* means "fullness, abundance," *cālpu* means "excellence, nobility" (*Ibid*: 18). So, in his dictum, it means 'a complete man/a whole man/a perfect man.' And he adds: "The world exists because noble and cultured men exist; without them, the world would vanish in dust" (*Ibid*). He elaborates furthermore: "The ideal of human life was to be achieved in this life; and it was the ideal of a wise man of human proportions and with human qualities. The important fact is that this Tamil wise men, the *cāṉṟōṉ* is not an anchorite or a recluse, not an ascetic of any kind and shade, but a man of flesh and blood who should live fully his days of courtship and of married life, of fighting and love-making, rejoicing in the laughter and happiness with his children and friends and fully dedicated to his social and civic duties" (*Ibid.,* p. 17). Undoubtedly, the term *cāṉṟōṉ* has been widely interpreted to signify *a noble man.* But we should know that the qualities/interpretations attributed to the word arguably do vary from time to time. Evidently, the period of the Sangam works is the last phase of the 'Heroic Age.' During this period, it was primarily *the warriors* who actually commanded the great respect of kings and then society. It is apparent that the word mostly and specifically referred to *warriors.* However, very rarely in the corpus of Sangam poems, the noun *cāṉṟōr* refers to *noble men* (in the moral sense) too. A metrical line from one of the poems (191) of *Puṟanāṉūṟu* is adjoined with a unit of adjective *koḷgai* (principled) which possibly means the aforesaid qualities.

When someone wonders: "How come the poet Picirāndaiyār does not have grey hair despite being full of years!" Then the poet mentions the following reasons: "I am so fortunate that my wife is virtuous; my offspring are full of understanding; my servants do what I wish; the King desists from doing unrighteous actions and protects his subjects and the place where I live has full of *ānravindu aḍangiya koḷgaic cānrōr* (the great men principled in their mature wisdom, humility and self-contained)."

> If you ask me,
> "You have lived for many years.
> Why is your hair not white?,"
> it is because my wife is virtuous,
> my children have gone far in learning,
> my servants do what I wish
> and my king protects, not doing
> what should not be done?
>
> Also, in my town, there are many noble
> men who are wise and have self-control!
>
> (Picirāndaiyār, *Puranānūru* 191, tr. Vaidehi Herbert)[7]

Thus, the noun phrase *ānravindu aḍangiya koḷgaic cānrōr* contextually means 'the wise men or the men of virtues.'

Cānrōn in Tirukkuṛaḷ (*c.* 250 CE): Learned/Wise/Noble Man

While the mothers of the 'Sangam Age' felt proud to have their sons skilled in warfare, the mothers in the post-Sangam period also had the same sense of pride but for a different reason, i.e., for being *sagacious* or *wise.* Let us see how a mother bearing a wise son feels proud in the following *Tirukkuṛaḷ*:[8]

> The mother who hears her son called "a wise man" will rejoice more than she did at his birth.
>
> (*TKḶ* 69, trs. Drew & Lazarus 1989: 15)

This is the happiest feeling of the mother juxtaposed to that of the mother of the Sangam poem (*PNU* 278) stated earlier. Nevertheless, the sons in both instances are yet denoted by the same term *cāṉṟōṉ* but with different connotations (*a warrior* in the Sangam poem but *a wise man* in the *TKḶ*). Any woman in family life will certainly feel immensely happy when she bears a child. (It is so if the offspring [especially the first one] happens to be a male child in the Indian context now). It is observed elsewhere that womanhood becomes full/complete only with motherhood. A woman undergoes unbearable/indescribable *labour pain* while giving birth to a child. However, all her horrifying pains will vanish at once as she (the mother) just glances at her newborn child. This instantly makes her feel exultant. For mothers of the post-Sangam period, the most rejoicing moment occurs at hearing her son as *a wise man* (of learned-wisdom-noble qualities) of impeccable qualities. When the bygone society of Tiruvaḷḷuvar days started degenerating at individual as well as societal levels, wise men of noble attributes were indeed essential for its well-being and existence. TVR feels that only education drives humanity into the path of righteousness. He denotes all those people of righteousness only with the term *cāṉṟōr*[9] (*aram poruḷ kaṇḍār*, 'those who know the attributes of virtue and wealth,' *TKḶ* 141), (*āṉṟa periyar*, 'the august men,' *TKḶ* 694) in his couplets wherever required. According to the versifier's opinion, *cāṉṟōṉ* is a man who does not indulge in any sort of immoral activity in any situation. Usually, no man stomachs his mother starving in hunger. Even in such a bad scenario of emotional upset, the poet opines: "The son should refrain from any action condemned by *cāṉṟōr*" ('the learned people,' *TKḶ* 656).

> *īṉṟāḷ pacikāṇbāṉ āyiṉum ceyyaṟka*
> *cāṉṟōr paḻikkum viṉai.*   (*TKḶ* 656)

Here the term *cāṉṟōr* connotes contextually *the learned*. It is because only education makes people become aware of what is good or bad/right or wrong to progress in their lives. Only those people adhering to *dharma* (righteousness/virtue) handle the case of a dispute without prejudice just like *tulākkōl*, "the rod of the balancing equal scale" (*TKḶ* 118). "Only such great people do not lead an immoral life as they are very sensitive to shame. They are very much aware of the truth that adversity and prosperity do happen respectively due to the destiny of good and bad acts" (*TKḶ* 115). "Only these great men of nobility have the magnanimous manliness of not desiring another man's wife" (*TKḶ* 148). Thus, it shows how the term *cāṉṟōr* connoted in general meaning but differently from the Sangam poems as *the learned, the great men,* and *the noble men.* It is in the same aforesaid sense, the term is rendered in all other post-Sangam works including the *Nālaḍiyār*[10] as a shift has taken place in the culture of Tamiḻs due to the excesses of absolute powerful kings.

II

Nōkku: Sight of Love/Gaze > Looking

It is a common feature that all languages have synonyms. Evidently, we can find countless synonyms in the Tamiḻ language too. For instance, let us consider the pair of verbs: *Ī-Tā-Koḍu* ("Grant-Provide-Give"). Though these terms seem to denote the same meaning at surface level, they have very subtle differences at deeper level. From the position of a speaker to someone, these terms do actually mean different things. The first term 'ī' contextually denotes *a kind of begging or requesting.* Essentially, it is *a plea* from a periphery to a centre. This is the expression of an inferior by age, wealth, class and so on. Whereas the last term *koḍu* imparts altogether a different meaning. Etymologically expressing *give*, the term becomes *a word of order/command*. The order is the expression of a superior. But juxtaposed to the aforesaid two terms, the middle term '*tā*' seemingly means *provide*. This is the expression between equals.

Similarly, three infinitives that are under our discussion are: *Pār-Kāṇ-Nōkku*. These verbal roots may be translated in English as *See–View–Look*. Consequently, they become verbal nouns denoting certain actions such as *pārttal* (seeing)—*kāṇal/kāṇudal* (viewing)—*nōkkal/nōkkudal* (looking/gazing). Evidently, there exist subtle differences in the meanings of these words. While *seeing* anything ordinarily without any seriousness is denoted by the term *pārttal* (seeing), *viewing* something/someone consciously with interest is *kāṇal/kāṇudal* (viewing) but *looking* at the same with deep involvement is *nōkkal/nōkkudal* (looking/gazing). Of *pār-kāṇ-nōkku* terms, the first two are rendered exclusively as verbs, whereas the last one functions both as a verb and a noun but in different contexts.

Observing someone or something with deep interest and involvement is known as *nōkku/nōkkal/nōkkudal* (look/looking). But actually, the prevailing meaning seems to have derived from the term *nōkku/nōkkam* (sight of love/gaze) rendered in several poems of classical Tamiḻ works. Needless to say, 'the sight of love' holds both the lover and the beloved so closely, as they fall in love and mutually become interested in each other with true fondness. Thus, in the sense of *sight of love/gaze*, the term *nōkku* has been rendered in several Sangam poems and *Tirukkuṟaḷ* couplets[11] (except the *TKḶ* couplet 1047).

We can further understand its connotation through the phrase *pēdai maḍanōkkam,* 'the meek looks of innocent girl'— as referred to in *Paripāḍal* (Kuṉram Bhūdaṉār, *PPL* 9: 48), an anthology of hymns. Since pre-historic times, men have typically been the ones to fall in love and express it openly, often gazing women with deep emotional involvement. Women, on the other hand, true to their natural attributes of meekness, shyness and modesty, tend not to respond immediately to such *gazes*. Even when they feel liking, they often hesitate to look directly at their beloveds, and are generally reluctant to express their love openly.

Let us see how this delicate nature of women is aesthetically portrayed in the following *Tirukkuṟaḷ* couplet.

> *yāṉ nōkkuṅkāl nilaṉōkkum nōkkākkāl*
> *tāṉōkki mella nagum.*   (*TKḶ* 1094)

> I look; she droops to earth awhile
> I turn; she looks with gentle smile.

(tr. Bharati 2008: 224)

This is a couplet expressed/essayed through the hero. We could see how the unique term *nōkku* (the sight of love/gaze) is employed four times (in the couplet of seven metrical units) conveying the body language of the hero and his sweetheart. When he *looks/gazes/throws intense sight of love* (*nōkku*) at her, true to her shyness/modesty she casts her look to the earth. When he does not, she *gazes/looks/throws intense sight of love* at him with docile and smiles gently. *Usually, a man has no qualms to look passionately at a girl/lady/woman of his liking whereas a woman has prevailed by her psyche.*

Having fallen in love with a girl and bewitched by the beauty of her eyes, a man gets love-sickness. Subsequently, he gets puzzled over her 'intense sight of love' (*nōkku*) tossed by her eyes which slay him as the 'God of Death' can do with a sharp tool; yet, at the same time, her eyes become sheepish and docile as doe does, out of shyness. In order to denote *the slaying, mobile, and docile nature of the eyes of the woman* who is possessed of love feelings—the following couplet aesthetically essays the piercing yet timid looks of the girl in the following manner.

> *kūṟṟamō kaṇṇō piṇaiyō maḍavaral*
> *nōkkamim mūṉṟu muḍaittu.*   (*TKḶ* 1085)

> Is it Yama, (a pair of) eyes or a hind?—Are not
> all these three in the looks of this maid?

> (trs. Drew & Lazarus 1989: 219)

It is true that the men who fall in love feel sick due to the penetrating eyes of their sweethearts. And they get cured by the same eyes that soothe the pain subsequently. Thus, their *nōkku,* 'the passionate gaze,' initially induces a sickness of desire but eventually transforms into the very cure. This dual role of *the passionate look of a girl's eyes* is thus seemingly termed with the word *nōkku* thrice in the following couplet.

> *irunōkku ivaḷuṇkaṇ uḷḷadu orunōkku*
> *nōynōk koṉṟannōy marundu.*   (*TKḶ* 1091)

> There are two looks in the dyed eyes of this (fair one),
> one causes pain, and the other is the cure thereof.

> (trs. Drew & Lazarus 1989: 221)

Another hero has become bewitched by the captivating beauty of one heroine. He *gazed/intensely looked at* her for quite some time. To his surprise, the charming, voluptuous damsel has responded to his *looking* more passionately than his. Though she is alone, she appears that she has come with a battalion of army to strike him. We notice that (the intense passionate) *looks/ gazes* of the couple are denoted with the same term *nōkku* thrice in the following couplet.

> *nōkkiṉāṉ ṉōkkedir nōkkudal tākkaṇangu*
> *tāṉaik koṇḍaṉṉa duḍaittu.*   (*TKḶ* 1082)

> This female beauty returning my looks is like
> a celestial maiden coming with an army to contend against me.
> (trs. Drew & Lazarus 1989: 219)

When the eyes of a lovelorn couple become *looked/gazed*, locked with each other, the words of their mouths are of no use. Here in the following couplet too, *the intense love-look* is again denoted with the term *nōkku*.

> *kaṇṇoḍu kaṇṇiṇai nōkkokkiṉ vāyccoṟkaḷ*
> *eṉṉa payaṉu mila.*   (*TKḶ* 1100)

> The words of mouth are of no use
> When eye to eye agrees the gaze.

> (tr. Bharati 2008: 225)

Kambaṉ, a prodigious Tamiḻ poet, has employed intact these two catchy words *kaṇṇoḍu kaṇṇiṇai* in his classic epic *Kamba Rāmāyaṇam*. These two terms appearing in a poem have become so popular in Tamiḻ literary discourses even nowadays. As we know, Vālmīki, a celebrated poet who originally penned the *Rāmāyaṇa* in Sanskrit, has not portrayed Rāma and Sīta as known to each other before the event of the 'breaking of the bow.' But Kambaṉ, who rendered its adaptation in Tamiḻ, crafted little change in the sequence of events so fittingly only to adhere to the ancient Tamiḻ *aham* convention. It may be mentioned here that Tolkāppiyar (*c.* 300 BCE), the earliest Tamiḻ grammarian, had outlined the features of Tamiḻ love convention in his grammatical treatise *Tolkāppiyam*. He delineates: "By the command of God, a man (lover) and woman (ladylove) being equal in status meet together and get married after their courtship" (*TKM,* "Poruḷadigāram," Kaḷaviyal 2, *cf.* Ilakkuvanar 1963: 175); "Solemnizing their courtship is said to be that the 'would-be husband' will have his 'would-be-wife' being given by those who are legally entitled to do so with the usual ceremony. Their marriage will take place even without the givers when they (bridegroom and bride) resort to elopement" (*TKM,* "Poruḷadigāram," Karpiyal 1–2, *cf.* Ilakkuvanar, *Ibid.,* p. 189). So, accordingly, the Kamban has depicted a situation where Rāma and Sīta see each other and fall in love before the event of 'breaking the bow.' Along with Rāma and Lakshmaṇa, a great seer Vishwāmitra enters Mithila city. While proceeding to the royal place of King Janaka, incidentally, Rāma *looked* up at the balcony of the palace where Sīta was standing. She too did *look at* him simultaneously. Instantly their eyes met and mingled. He *gazed/glanced* (*nōkku*) *at* her; she too *gazed/glanced at* him. They exchanged their glances. And at that very moment, their hearts were united too. Instantaneously, love cropped up between them in no time. Let us see how the ever great Tamil poet Kamban sketches the scene so amusingly here.

> *eṉṉaru nalattiṉāḷ iṉaiyaḷ niṉruḷi*
> *kaṇṇodu kaṇṇiṉaik kavvi oṉraiyoṉru*
> *uṇṇavum nilaiperādu uṇarvum oṉriḍa*
> *aṇṇalum nōkkiṉāṉ avaḷum nōkkiṉāḷ.*

> (*Kamba Rāmāyaṇam,* Bāla Kāṇḍam,
> "Midilaikkāṭcip Paḍalam" 35)

> As unimaginable beauty (Sīta) thus standing,
> the two pairs of eyes *devouring* each other;
> they delighted in eating each other; their awareness unsettled,
> the lord *looked* (at her); she too *looked* (at him).

> (tr. Vanathu Antoni)

Since the day Kamban presented his magnum opus before a learned assembly for its approval, the above-quoted word-picture has been ruling the roost in Tamil literary stages as well as ordinary conversations. Kamban eulogizes *the loving looks* of Rāma and Sīta. Rāma's eyes *fell* on Sīta and hers on him. "Their minds merged, and their feelings mingled," says Vai.

Mu. Gopala Krishnamachariyar (*Śrī Kamba Rāmāyaṇam*, "Bāla Kāṇḍam," 1965: 449). The explanation of the pen-picture goes thus: "As Sīta with unimaginable beauty stood thus, their eyes *devoured* each other. They delighted in eating with each other. Their awareness was unsettled and their hearts mingled. Rāma cast his *deep loving look* on Sīta. Simultaneously she too cast her *deep loving look* on him."

Thus, the term *nōkku*, originally connoted in the sense of *the intense sight of love* in *Tirukkuṟaḷ* (*c.* 250 CE) did sail (in the same meaning) up to the period of *Kamba Rāmāyaṇam* (*c.* 1200 CE) for one millennium years. It is heartening to know that Kambaṉ has upheld the ancient Tamiḻ love convention so intact even after centuries and narrated it so vividly. He has placed the highly evolved literary tradition so fittingly in his enduring epic for its poise and grace. It is only after the age of *Kamba Rāmāyaṇam* that the term *nōkku* seems to have evolved the meaning of *observing/looking* at something/someone seriously or with deep involvement. Thus, the term becomes a tool to proclaim an ancient Tamiḻ literary love convention.

III

Naṭpu: Love (Sexual Relationship) > (Usual) Friendship

Another unique term being rendered since Sangam poems till date post-modern Tamiḻ writings is *naṭpu*. It is commonly used at present to denote *the normal* or *close friendship* between people of same the sex (i.e., between male and male or female and female) irrespective of age, profession, status, caste, creed etc. But the term had been rendered specifically to refer to *kādal, the emotion of love/the sexual relationship* prevailing among the opposite sexes, i.e., between adults or matured male and female in the *aham* poems of Sangam classics.

The term *naṭpu,* the derivative of *naṇbu,* means "friendship." The Tamil word *naṇbaṉ* (*naṇbu+aṉ,* a suffix for singular masculine gender), denoting *a male friend,* is, actually, derived from the aforesaid noun. It is similar to the term *aṉbu* (affection) + *aṉ* that becomes *aṉbaṉ* (well-wisher). It is interesting to know that the term *naṇbu* denotes *the romantic relationship of hero and heroine* in *aham* ("interior feelings") poems whereas the same had been referring to "friendship" between males in *puram* ("exterior actions") poems. For instance, the following *Ahanāṉūru* poem shows how the term *naṇbu* is rendered in the sense of *romantic relationship* that usually exists between a man and a woman.

> ....
>
> *uravuppeyal poḻinda nallen yāmattu*
> *aravin paintalai iḍarip pāṇāḷ*
> *iravin vandem iḍaimulai muyangit*
> *tuṇikaṉ agala vaḷaiik kangulin*
> *iṉidiṉ iyainda* **naṇbavar** (lover) *muṇidal*
> *teṟṟā gudalnar karindaṉa māyiṉ*
> *ilanguvaḷai ñegiḻap parandupaḍar alaippayām*
> *muyangutoṟum muyangutoṟum uyanga mugandukoṇḍu*
> *aḍakkuvam maṉṉō tōḻi* ...
>
> ....
>
> *cāral nāḍaṉ cāyal mārbē!*
>
> (Iḷandēvaṉār, *Ahanāṉūru* 328,
>
> the emphasis and parenthesis are added by the author)

We could perceive the specific meaning of the term *naṇbu* in the following English rendering:

> It has become clear, the hatred
> of the man who came in the middle
> of the night, stumbling on the heads
> of bloody snakes, with deep friendship (love),
> who hugged me sweetly for my sorrow

to leave, in the mountain range with
surapunnai trees, where clouds rise
up to the sky on the right side and roar
loudly like the drums of drummers,
and come down as heavy rains.

Oh friend! Had I known this,
I who was distressed, my bright
bangles slipping down, would have
embraced again and again, hurting
the delicate chest of the man from
the mountains where clouds float,
where a naïve female elephant that
has given birth to her first calf eats
bamboo, and is lovingly stroked by
her mate, as she sleeps in the
beautiful mountain with banana trees.

(tr. Vaidehi Herbert,[12]
the parenthesis is added by the author)

The hero had been secretly and frequently meeting his beloved during nightfalls in the monsoon season, in a mountainous region. During this time, clouds would rise with force and roar like beaten drums before releasing heavy rains. The sudden, relentless thunder would strike the tender heads of snakes, ultimately causing their death. Undeterred, the hero continued to visit her, often stumbling over the bodies of these snakes during the downpours, to enjoy blissful nocturnal encounters. However, one day, he abruptly stopped coming—for reasons unknown. Yet the heroine (along with her *tōḻi*) awaits at the spot where she met him earlier in the dead of night. Thereupon, she becomes anxious. In this apprehensive milieu, she recalls his earlier *deep emotive relationship* (love) with her confidante by referring to him as *naṇbavar* (lover he/he, the lover).

Contrary to this connotation, the term *nanbu* has been rendered denoting generally *the usual friendship* in *Puranānūru*. For example, *igalvilan iniyan yātta nanbinan* (He never hurts, pleasant man, intimate friend), (Kōpperuñcōlan, *PNU* 216: 6), *cirumanai vālkkaiyin orīi varunarkku/ udavi yārru nanbir panbudai/ ūlir rāganin ceygai* (May your actions be friendly to those who come to your home in need), (Uraiyūr Mudukannan Cāttanār, *PNU* 29: 20–21). Thus, we see how the term *nanbu* on the one hand denotes *the love relationship* in *aham* poems while on the other in the sense of *friendship* in some *puram* poems.

The aforesaid term had been rendered also in several couplets of *Tirukkural* with the connotation of *friendship*. For example:

> *anbīnum ārvam udaimai aduvīnum*
> *nanbennum nādāc cirappu.*   (*TKL* 74)

> Love yields aspiration and thence
> Friendship springs up in excellence.

> (tr. Bharati 2008: 17)

Here in the *Tirukkural*, we could understand how the term *nanbu* (appearing as the first word in the second line) apparently refers to *friendship*. The couplet pronounces: "Love begets enthusiasm which in turn yields friendship of excellence with everyone especially." Even towards those of an unfriendly nature (*nanbarrār*), one must remain friendly—that is the mark of the noble. Otherwise, discourtesy becomes the blemish, regardless of one's greatness. This is the message explicitly imparted in the following couplet. So, *nanbu* (the first word appearing in the first line of the couplet), plainly means *friendship* which is added with the suffix *arrār*, 'those who lack.'

naṇbaṟṟā rāgi nayamila ceyvārkkum
paṇpaṟṟā rādal kaḍai.   (TKĻ 998)

In the Tamiḻ vocabulary, there exists a sequence of words as *tōḻamai* (friendship)—*tōḻaṇ* (male friend), *tōḻi* (female friend). But there exists no such sequence of words in the case of root words like *naṇbu* (friendship) and *aṇbu* (affection) to denote female categories: *Naṇbu* (friendship)—*naṇbaṇ* (male friend☑)—*naṇbaḷ/naṇbi* (female friend☒); *Aṇbu* (affection)—*aṇbaṇ* (male well-wisher☑)—*aṇbaḷ/aṇbi* (female well-wisher☒). When suffixes such as *'aṇ'* and *'ar'* denoting masculine gender singular and plural respectively adjoin the aforesaid root words (*naṇbu* and *aṇbu*), either *'aḷ,'* a suffix or *'i,'* a syllable denoting the feminine gender singular, does not exist, neither in colloquial nor in written language.

In *Kuṟuntogai* (*KRT*) anthology, a man meets a beautiful lady in the *kuṟiñci* (mountain) tract. Instantly, he falls in love with her. Ultimately, he desires to take her. However, the lady hesitates out of modesty. Yet, he does not give up hope. Thereafter, he decides to shoo away her shyness by gently touching her body parts. Nevertheless, he becomes captivated by the fragrance of her tresses. So, he enquires from a honeybee as follows: "O beautiful winged bee gathering honey from a cluster of flowers! Have you ever come across a most fragrant flower than the sweet-smelled tresses of my ladylove who keeps *naṭpu* (deep love relationship) unceasingly for births with me?"

konguṭēr vāḻkkai añciṟait tumbi
kāmam ceppādu kaṇḍadu moḻimō
payiliyadu keḻīiya naṭpiṇ mayiliyal
ceṟiyeyiṟ ṟarivai kūndaliṇ
naṟiyavum uḷavō nīyaṟiyum pūvē!

(Iṟaiyaṇār, *Kuṟuntogai* 2)

Here in the poem, the term *naṭpu* (appearing in the third line) does actually denote *the strong emotive relationship*, viz. 'love' (the unique feeling and emotive relationship that naturally exists between the opposite sexes) but not in the modern-day connotation of *normal relationship*. It is noteworthy that the hero (the speaker in the poem) emphasizes his sweetheart's enduring love across many births with the term *naṭpu*, denoting *the emotional love*. This particular term as well as the poem has been rendered perfectly into English in the following manner.

> O beautiful, winged bee
> whose life is choosing honey!
> Tell me what you found and not
> what pleases me!
> Is there a flower with more
> fragrance than the hair of my
> beloved woman with perfect teeth,
> peacock nature and enduring love?
>
> (tr. Vaidehi Herbert)[13]

Also, in another poem from the same anthology but put through the mouth of a heroine, the term *naṭpu* is again rendered exactly in the same meaning of *emotional love* that usually exists between a man and a woman.

> *nilattiṉum peridē vāṉiṉum uyarndaṉru*
> *nīriṉum āraḷa viṉṟē cāral*
> *karuṅkōl kuṟiñcip pūkkoṇḍu*
> *peruntēṉ iḷaikkum nāḍaṉoḍu naṭpē!*
>
> (Dēvakulattār, *Kuṟuntogai* 3)

The heroine in the aforesaid poem does use the same term *naṭpu* while she is delightfully referring to *the bigger, higher and more unfathomable love relationship* that exists between herself and her man. But she emphasizes her *deep emotive relationship* with the term *naṭpē* ('*ē*' is a metrical syllable that emphasizes the given word). Let us see, how the term and the poem are rendered so poetically into English here.

> Bigger than earth, certainly,
> higher than the sky,
> more unfathomable than the waters
> is this love (*naṭpē!*) for this man
>
>> of the mountain slopes
>> where bees make rich honey
>> from the flowers of the *kuṟiñci*
>> that has such black stalks.
>
> (tr. Ramanujan 1985: 5,
>
> the parenthesis is added by the author)

"The poem opens with large abstractions about her love" (Ramanujan 1985: 244). Understandably, her *naṭpu* (enduring intense love) with the man is bigger than the earth, higher than the sky and deeper than the ocean. This is the overwhelming blissful relationship a woman like her can cherish. It is often in the sense of denoting such *everlasting deep sensual love relationship of man and woman*, the aforesaid unique term has been rendered strikingly in several poems of Sangam classics.[14] For example,

> *amma vāḻi tōḻi nammoḍu*
> *piriviṉ ṟāyiṉ naṉṟumaṉ tilla*
> ....
> *vilangumalai nāḍaṉoḍu kalanda naṭpē!*
>
> (Kōvēngaip Peruṅkadavaṉār, *Kuṟuntogai* 134)

A heroine fears that her man from the mountain region is contemplating going away from her for some reason. She has already given herself completely to him and emotionally become attached to him. So, she wishes, "her deep perpetual intermingled love relationship with the man from a mountain region" (*malai nāḍanoḍu kalanda naṭpu*) should not see any setback. That is what she aspires; she feels that only this would be enough for her. In this poem also, '*ē*'—a metrical syllable is adjoined to the term *naṭpu* (> *naṭpē*) only to emphasize *the enduring love relationship* of a man and a woman. The following metrical lines would testify to the nuances of her enduring love feelings and sentiment.

> May you live long, my friend!
> It would be nice
> if there is no parting
> from this union of love (*kalanda naṭpu*)
> with the man
> from the blocking mountains.
>
> (tr. Vaidehi Herbert,[15]
> the parenthesis is added by the author)

In the following metrical lines, the term *naṭpu* is further stated more vividly and expressed splendidly with a similar term *kādal*. The latter term has replaced the former for centuries, fully usurped its connotation and is being expressed in Tamiḻ literary writings as well as in its ordinary day-to-day language in the sense of a *long-lasting intermingled love relationship* found between man and woman. Let us observe how the following stanzas describe the delicate difference between the enduring love and passing the short-time passion of a man and a woman.

> *uyiriyain daṉṉa naṭpiṉ avvuyir*
> *vāḻdal aṉṉa kādal*
> *cādal aṉṉa pirivaṟi yōḷē!*
>
> (Naraimuḍi Neṭṭimaiyār, *Ahanāṉūṟu* 339: 12–14)

The terms *naṭpu* and *kādal* rendered in the poem are no doubt synonyms but with a subtle difference—denoting the typical emotional relationship of man and woman. Evidently, here **naṭpu refers to *an everlasting emotional bond* or *soul-mingled relationship* often found among well-mannered men and women whereas *kādal* denotes their *momentary/short-lived passion.*** We can grasp the subtle difference of these terms in the following stanzas.

> Love is to living what beautiful life
> is to the body. Separation from the
> precious woman is like death!
>
> (tr. Vaidehi Herbert)[16]

The term *naṭpu* exceptionally in one *Ahanāṉūṟu* poem (195) refers to 'the umbilical relationship of mother and daughter' as *maḍanallāḷai īṉṟa naṭpu* (the relationship of having given birth to the naïve girl like doe-like looks).[17] Here, we can understand that their relationship too is an emotional and ever-lasting one like that of a man and a woman. Yet, they are different. The relationship between mother and daughter is genetic, natural and *pure affection* whereas man's *'love'* crops up over the latter's physical and mental beauty and charm.

In the post-Sangam literary works like *Tirukkuṟaḷ*, the cultural term *naṭpu*[18] has been often rendered with the aforesaid specific connotation. Also, the term has become the title of two chapters (79 & 80) of *Tirukkuṟaḷ* namely "Naṭpu" (Friendship), "Naṭpārāydal" (Choice of Friends). Strikingly, in one of the couplets, a husband refers to *the everlasting emotional bond* or *soul mingled relationship* of his wife with the term *naṭpu.* The bond is so profound/deeply rooted like the inseparable relationship that typically remains between body and soul, thus he speaks.

> *uḍamboḍu uyiriḍai eṉṉa marṟarṟa*
> *maḍandaiyoḍu emmiḍai naṭpu.*   (*TKḼ* 1122)

In another couplet under the chapter titled "Nilaiyāmai" (Instability) too the author Tiruvaḷḷuvar employs the same analogy mentioned above. He describes *the intimate-inseparable relationship of body and soul to the liking of a bird and egg-shells relationship.* Let us see the couplet with its translation as follows:

> *kuḍambai taṉittoḻiyap puḷparan daṟṟē*
> *uḍamboḍu uyiriḍai naṭpu.*   (*TKḶ* 338)

> The soul from body any day
> Like bird from egg-shell flies away.

> (tr. Bharati 2008: 69).

Contrarily, the term in our discussion, has also been rarely referring to *normal friendship of affection* which usually remains between adults of the same sex.

> Friendship (*naṭpu*) hastens help in mishaps
> Like hands picking up dress that slips.

> (*TKḶ* 788, tr. Bharati 2008: 161)

> Friendship (*naṭpu*) is not mere smile on face
> It is the smiling heart's embrace.

> (*TKḶ* 786, tr. Bharati 2008: 161,
> the parentheses are added by the author)

Thus, Tiruvaḷḷuvar defines friendship with the term *naṭpu* so profoundly and agreeably to the liking and appreciation of everyone regardless of time and place. He affirms: "Noble men will remember throughout their seven-fold births the friendship of willing friend who wiped out their tears" (*TKḶ* 107).

It is remarkable to show that some nouns such as *keḻutagaimai,*[19] *kēṇmai,*[20] *toḍarbu,*[21] and *toḍargai* (*TKḶ* 450), and verbal nouns such as *naṭṭal* (*TKḶ* 784 & 791), *paḻagudal* (*TKḶ* 785) have also been denoting the meaning of the term *naṭpu, the ever-*

lasting inseparable love relationship. Among these terms, *kēn-mai* has been rendered frequently in the exact meaning of *the everlasting emotional bond or soul-mingled relationship of well-mannered man and woman* pen-pictured in Sangam poems. For example, *kunra nāḍan kēnmai* (*KRT* 38 & 90), *malaikelu nāḍan kēnmai* (*KRT* 170), *sūrmalai nāḍan kēnmai* (*KRT* 105), and *poygai ūran kēnmai* (*KRT* 61). While the noun phrases, *kunra nāḍan, malaikelu nāḍan* and *sūrmalai nāḍan*—all refer to the lord of a mountain, the other noun phrase *poygai ūran* refers to the lord of cultivable lands filled with natural ponds. These noun phrases referring to *the everlasting deep soul-mingled relationship* (intense love relationship) of man are stated either by the heroine or by her confidante in those poems. It is imperative that the women personae depicted in *aham* poems render this term exactly in the sense of *natpu* (everlasting inseparable love relationship) as stated earlier.

Though the aforesaid term occurs in several of *Tirukkural* couplets, it is not in the above-mentioned meaning. But it is rendered referring to *the normal caring friendship which usually remains between adults of the same sex.* These two terms (*kēnmai* and *natpu*) have been rendered in a few couplets that describe the subtle difference that rests between them. We can comprehend the difference or nuance of these words as expressed in the following couplet.

> *maravarka mācarrār kēnmai turavarka*
> *tunbattul tuppāyār natpu.*   (*TKL* 106)

Forget not "the friendship" (*kēnmai*) of pure people.
Forsake not "the friendship" (*natpu*) of those—
    who stood by you in adverse times.

(The translation and parenthesis are by the author)

Though both terms denote similar meanings, they are not connoting the same. It may be otherwise stated: "Forgetting the friendship of perfect people is not good; forsaking the friendship of people who render timely help is bad." The former would not bring any daunting ill-reputation to the person who forget the friendship of immaculate people whereas the latter would surely have a terrible effect on him/her sometimes later. This is what the couplet states explicitly—what one should do in the matter of friendship. Evidently, we can comprehend the slight difference that persists between these two terms. No doubt, *naṭpu* is truly significant than *kēṇmai* though they both denote similar meanings. This same notion is shown differently in the following couplet: "Friendship developed with noble and wise men will grow day by day like the waxing moon, whereas the friendship with illiterate fools will diminish day by day like the waning moon" (Viswanathan 2011: 238).

> *niṟainīra nīravar kēṇmai piṟaimadip*
> *piṉnīra pēdaiyār naṭpu.*   (*TKḶ* 782)

> The friendship of the wise waxes like the new moon
> (but) that of fools wanes like the full moon.

> (tr. Drew & Lazarus 1989: 159).

Needless to say, the friendship (*kēṇmai*) of wise men gradually progresses like the new moon only to mature as a full moon later. Whereas the friendship (*naṭpu*) of unwise men seemingly full at the beginning slowly fades away later as the full moon dwindles into mere dark shades. Tiruvaḷḷuvar thus employs these two terms splendidly in analogy to refer to two kinds of friendship. Apparently, in this couplet of *Tirukkuraḷ*, the author places *naṭpu* on a higher pedestal than *kēṇmai*. The former gradually matures into bloom whereas the latter slowly lessens into gloom. The friendship of wise/learned/upright people usually progresses steadily over a period of time. Thereby it remains intimate and intact for a longer period. Whereas the friendship of unwise/unlearned/immoral people starts rousingly at the beginning but sooner or later disappears as bubbles.

Though there is no separate Tamil term to denote *a friend* in *Tirukkural,* there are some terms generally referring to *friends* (plural nouns) such as *kēnmaiyār* (*TKL* 809), *kēnmaiyavar* (*TKL* 807), *kiḷaiñar* (*TKL* 796), *naṭṭār*[22] in the line of *tōlar/naṇbar* (male friends). From the pieces of evidence we have cited, we may pertinently conclude that **the cultural term *naṭpu* has been rendered in several of Sangam poems as well as in a few couplets of *Tirukkural* specifically denoting *the emotional love union of man and woman* and yet rarely referring to the *normal* or *close friendship* of same the sex.**

IV

***Virundu*: Novelty/Newness/
Unknown People/Strangers > Feast**

Another exceptional term that affirms the cultural mobility of Tamils is *virundu.* The real meaning of the term was novelty/newness or new or unknown person(s)/stranger(s). But nowadays the term is being rendered in the sense of feast or dinner. Etymologically, it means a new variety of food items that supposedly taste afresh for the guests. Since, fresh food items are usually served in social gatherings like *tirumaṇam* (wedding), *cigai nīkku-kādaṇi viḷā* (tonsure-cum-ear boring function), *upanayana* ceremony (a sanctifying ritual [*samskāra*] of wearing the sacred thread to *brāhmiṇ* boys mostly at the age of five), *mañcal nīrāṭṭu viḷā/pūppuc caḍangu viḷā* (bathing ceremony of (a girl) attaining puberty), etc., and festivals like *pongal, dīpāvaḷi, kārttigai dīpam,* etc., the new food items are denoted with the aforesaid term as *virundu.* This is the common meaning of the term which has been in vogue for ages. In this connotation, the term was rendered only in a few poems of Sangam classics. For example, *virunduṇ ḍāṉāp peruñcōr ṟaṭṭil* (Kaḍiyalūr Urittiraṅkaṇṇaṉār, *Paṭṭiṉappālai,* line 262), (the guests ate the feast unlimited big meal made in the kitchen), *vacaiyil vāṉtiṇaip puraiyōr kaḍumboḍu/ virunduṇ ḍeñciya miccil peruntagai/ niṉṉoḍu uṇḍalum puraivadu* (after the wise, rich and relatives have eaten their stomach full, we will eat together the left-over food. A noble one, eating with you will be special), (Kabilar, *Kuṟiñcippāṭṭu,* lines 205–07). The aforesaid stanzas seemingly attest to a fact about the ancient Tamiḻs' culture wherein fresh food varieties were served to the gatherings on special occasions.

Strikingly, the term *virundu* occurs for the very first time absolutely in the sense of novelty/newness in the second part of *Tolkāppiyam* titled "Colladigāram" (Kiḷaviyākkam 56) which deals with etymology, morphology, semantics and syntax. The term again occurs in the third part of the same grammatical work titled "Poruḷadigāram" (Ceyyuḷiyal 231) which mainly deals with poetics. While the grammarian is explaining the concept called *virundu* in the chapter "Ceyyuḷiyal," he says, *virundē tāṉum, puduvadu puṇainda yāppiṉ mēṟṟē (virundu* is a kind of verse speaking new ideas in a new way).

It is in the same connotation as *newness,* the term is rendered in several Sangam poems. For example, *meliya rallōr virundupuṇa layara* (those who are strong enough advance into the new waters and play), (Nallanduvaṉār, *Paripāḍal* 6: 40). After the scorching summer days, rain finally arrived. People were instantly ecstatic, and some strong individuals rushed towards the river. They began playing in its 'fresh waters' and thoroughly enjoyed the sport. Hence, the poet Nallanduvaṉār meaningfully employs the term *virundupuṉal* just to refer to rainwater for its *newness*.

A feast or a special food is also denoted as *virundu* in some poems of Sangam works. A hero frequently sees and takes his ladylove at the usual meeting spot of 'day-tryst' (*pagaṟkuṟi*). His sweetheart wants him should marry her soon. So, her *tōḻi* asks him to go along with his servants by chariot to the heroine's home. She tells him to stay at her house as a stranger for some days to relish *the good feast*. Thereby, their wedding will be fixed without further delay. See these details seemingly are comprehended in the following poem (*ANU* 300).

> *iḷaiyarum puraviyum iṉbuṟa nīyum*
> *illuṟai nalvirundu ayardal*
> *olludal perumaṉī nalgudal peṟiṉē!*

(Ulōccaṉār, *Ahanāṉūṟu* 300: 20–22)

> With your horses and servants, you will be
> happier by enjoying our *nalvirundu*, ("good feast")
> if you agree to visit and stay at our house.

(tr. Author)

A hero, as depicted in the aforesaid anthology, is returning home from the battlefield after completing the mission successfully. His king's great rage has ebbed as the *new kings* have given their tributes to him. Sweet rain started falling with a loud uproar from the skies. Consequently, he asks his charioteer to drive the chariot fast so that he can see his wife early who awaits him with patience. In the poem (*ANU* 54), the poet Koṟṟaṅkoṟṟaṉār has rendered suitably the phrase *virundiṉ maṉṉar* just to refer to the *new kings* as they have not fought with him but accepted his prowess by paying tributes to him. Similarly, another hero also returned home after performing his stately duty successfully during the rainy season in the evening time. He also urges the charioteer to hasten the chariot only to have a blissful union with his wife. So, he asks the charioteer,

> *celga tērē nalvalam peruna!*
> *peruntōḷ nuṇugiya nucuppin*
> *tirundiḻai arivai virundedir koḷavē!*

(Iḍaikkāḍaṉār, *Ahanāṉūru* 374: 16–18)

> Drive the chariot (speedily), O highly skilled charioteer!
> so that I can have *virundu* ("the feast")
> from the young woman with wide shoulders,
> thin waist and perfect jewels.

(tr. Author)

The phrase *arivai virundu* (*arivai* = woman, *virundu* = feast) appearing in the last line of the poem conveys certain unique meanings. One is explicit while the other is implicit. Since the man is returning home after a long time, his wife awaits to treat him with a feast, the just-cooked tasty food items. We can infer its suggestive meaning by considering other phrases such as 'wide shoulders, thin waist and perfect jewels' of the young woman, the heroine. So, these words conspicuously mean that his wife will treat him *afresh* by offering herself a *feast*; and will entertain him sexually with innovative methods.

In another poem from the same anthology, the term thus appears and conveys a similar meaning. In this poem too, a hero is returning home after completing his mission in a chariot. On seeing him hurry in the chariot, some farm labourers whisper saying,

> *virundum perugunaḷ pōlum tirundiḻait*
> *taḍamen paṇaittōḷ maḍamoḻi arivai*

....
cellum neḍuntagai tērē
mullai mālai nagarpuga lāyndē!

(Okkūr Macāttiyār, *Ahanāṉūṟu* 324: 1–15)

perhaps, she will get a *virundu* ("feast")—
the woman wearing perfectly made jewels,
who is with soft bamboo-like shoulders,
and with a soft-spoken nature!
....
the chariot of the towering, esteemed man
going in this *mullai* tract
might enter the town in the evening!

(tr. Author)

Here too, the term occurs in the same connotation, i.e., *the blissful sexual union* but with a difference. Here, the hero becomes *the host* while his wife is *the guest*. He is about to treat her *afresh* by entertaining her sexually with vigour. We can understand now how the term *virundu* connotes *feast* etymologically as well as *something else* suggestively.

It is to be noted that the term is otherwise rendered in the sense of *new people/unknown people/strangers* in *Puranāṉūṟu*, an anthology of heroic poems. Once, the Cōḻa King Kuḷamuṟṟattut Tuñciya Kiḷḷivaḷavaṉ conquers his enemy Malaiyamāṉ in a battle. After eliminating him, he imprisons his little children along with others and brings them to his country only to kill them cruelly. In a public place, where numerous people have gathered, he buries them alive, leaving only their heads above the pits to allow the elephants to trample them underfoot. Coming to know about the imminent inhuman action, the poet Kōvūrkiḻār enters the scene at the right moment to save the innocent children. He counsels the cruel king with courage and conviction. He reminds him of his forefather's unique gesture shown to a pigeon out of compassion. He brings to his knowledge the benevolent attribute of the children's forefathers too. Further, in the end, he points out the innocent nature of those children. That finally changes the heart of the king. We can realize how the term *virundu* is employed in the poem to denote these children as *unknown people/strangers*.

> *kaḷirukaṇ ḍaḷum aḷāal maranda*
> *puntalaic ciṟāar maṉṟumaruṇḍu nōkki*
> *virundiṟ puṉkaṉṉō vuḍaiyar!*
> *kēṭṭaṉai yāyiṉṉī vēṭṭadu ceymmē!*

(Kōvūrkiḷār to Kiḷḷivaḷavaṉ, *Puṟanāṉūṟu* 46: 5–8)

....

> Look at these children,
> the crowns of their heads are still soft.
>
> As they watch the elephants,
> they even forget to cry,
> stare dumbstruck at the crowd
> in some new (*virundu*) terror
> of things unknown.
>
> Now that you've heard me out,
> do what you will.

(tr. Ramanujan 1985: 122, the parenthesis is added by the author)

The phrase *"virundiṉ puṉkaṇ nōvuḍaiyar"* needs to be understood here semantically. Since the enemy king's children are brought to *a new place*, and they see a lot of *new faces* gathered there for the first time and undergoing *a novel* thrilling experience, all these make them feel a *new terror* (*virundiṉ puṉkaṇ nōvuḍaiyar*). Thus, the term *virundu* has become a unique one connoting the *bewildered looks* of those children who have forgotten to cry now. It also refers to the pathetic situation of the children who see the *new crowds* and undergo *new distress* for the first time in their lives. Even the warriors who fought with bravery and died on battlefields are also referred to as *virundu* (*new people*) in another context.

> *arumperal ulagam niraiya*
> *virunduper ranarāl poliganum pugalē!*
>
> (Kalāttalaiyār, *Puranānūru* 62: 18–19)
>
> As the *virundu* ("new people") arrived and
> filled the other world (the heaven) that is so hard to obtain,
> they were treated as "new entrants" by the celestials there,
> may the glory of both of you glow!
>
> (tr. Author)

Since the warriors are believed to be the *new entrants* to heaven as other great/noble men do arrive at the unattainable place, they are also termed as *virundu, new persons/new entrants*. Exactly in the aforesaid meaning (new people/unknown people/strangers), the term in our discussion has been rendered in several couplets of *Tirukkural*[23] too.

However, nowadays even one's close relatives like maternal/paternal uncle, aunt, brother-in-law, sister-in-law, nephew, niece, and others are strangely referred to with the aforesaid term in modern Tamil culture. Denoted as *curram* in *Tolkāppiyam, kēlir/kilaiñar* in Sangam and *Tirukkural* works in ancient times; as *condam, bandam, currattinar, condakkārargal, uravu muraiyōr*, etc., (all just mean relatives) till recently in Tamil literary works as well as in spoken Tamil, these people are now being referred to as *virundu* or *virundinar* in the sense of *guests*. Apparently, a change in the meaning of the term had taken place since the arrival of the British and with the introduction of English education in Tamil Nadu.

Indian society, including Tamil ethnicity, is fundamentally *informal*. It is primarily built on emotionally connected and so tightly knit relationships among people. In Indian social culture, relatives, friends, and acquaintances cannot be referred to as *guests* (*virundu/virundinar*). However, in Western culture, the same individuals may be considered *guests*, as their society is regarded as *formal*. It is a well-established fact that private space is crucial and distinctly maintained between individuals, even among children and parents, in European culture.

It may be relevant here to evoke the expressions of Tolkāppiyar about the excellence of wife, 'the homemaker' in a chapter of his grammatical work (*Tolkāppiyam*, "Poruḷadigāram," Karpiyal 11). He says: "Chastity, love, good behaviour, patience of tender nature, magnanimity, entertaining the *virundu* (new people/unknown people) promptly and supporting the *curram* (relations), and such others are the excellences of the wife" (Ilakkuvanar, *Ibid.*, p. 196). From the above expression, we can comprehend how significant they were—well-treating the *strangers/outsiders/new people* and taking care of relatives—as they are basic characteristics of Tamils' family life. Tamils regard household life as the most virtuous ideal one can aspire to on this planet. As a result, such life has been given primary place in Tamils traditional culture for ages. The chief duty of the householder is not only taking care of his wife, and children but also *tenpulattār* (the souls of the deceased), *deyvam* (God), *virundu* (outsiders/strangers), *okkal* (relations) and at last *tān* (himself), (*TKL* 43). Household life is considered as the axis for the existence of the World. Hence, there are 200 couplets (in the first section of *Tirukkuraḷ*, i.e., from chapters 5 to 24) that talk about the greatness of domestic life. It is asserted that the whole exercise of leading a domestic life along with a wife on earth (by not being exiled to the forest) is only to extend hospitality to *virundu* (strangers/unknown people). This can be understood from the following couplet:

> *irundōmbi ilvālva dellām virundōmbi*
> *vēlānmai ceydar poruttu.*   (*TKL* 81)

> Men set up home, toil and earn
> To tend the guests and do good turn.

> (tr. Bharati 2008: 19)

We can see in the above translation, how the term *virundu* is misinterpreted as *guests*. The shift in its semantics is to be seen against the backdrop of the 'invasion of British culture' on Tamils. Ordinarily, *virundu* (> *virundinar*), the ancient Tamil term, is rendered nowadays exclusively in the connotation of the English term *guests*. But the term as rendered in ancient Tamil works like *Tirukkural* actually mean the people not known ever before even by face. So, what the term really denotes is the new people or strangers. In ancient times, only strangers/unknown people would stay outside one's home. Every house typically had at least one *tinnai* (a raised platform on either side of the main door) to provide temporary shelter for strangers, such as travelers, wanderers, or even beggars. A couplet says: "Even if it were the nectar of immortality, one (householder) should avoid consuming it alone while *virundu*, (some unknown person) staying outside the house" (*TKL* 82). Evidently, we can understand that the actual implication of the term occurs in the following couplet but is again misinterpreted as 'guests' by Shuddhananda Bharati.

> *virundu purattadāt tānundal cāvā*
> *marundeninum vēndarpār ranru.*   (*TKL* 82)

To keep out guests cannot be good
Albeit you eat nectar-like food.

(tr. Bharati 2008: 19)

We should take note of the phrase *virundu puṟattadā,* appearing in the first line of the couplet. The phrase literally means some unknown person(s) staying outside (of the house). So, any friend or relative who has access to move inside one's home cannot be termed *a guest* in its prevailing meaning. People like unknown sages, travellers, desolate, and beggars (never seen/met before) were the ones the term *virundu* refers to. Becoming a host and taking care of such unknown people's needs (mainly food) is what is termed as *virundōmbal* (entertaining the unknown people, i.e., 'the hospitality').

There are several couplets that eulogize one's hospitality. For instance, "the Goddess of wealth will delightfully reside in the house of a person who cheerfully entertains *nalvirundu* (good or worthy unknown people), (*TKL* 84). Needless to say, when *strangers/unknown people* visit us, obviously they feel shy and move with hesitation. To do away with their shyness, one needs to welcome them with a smiling face and entertain them with charming words, and hearty hospitality. Otherwise, even by a little indifferent glance, they would wither away. "They are like the delicate flower *aṇiccam* which withers out just by smelling. So, withers *virundu* (an unknown person) just by a wry-faced look (*TKL* 90). In entertaining any *unknown person*, one should not expect anything in return. The person who treats a stranger with no expectation, indeed, will turn up as *nalvirundu* (worthy newcomer) to the celestials after his life.

celvirun dōmbi varuvirundu pārttiruppāṉ
nalvirundu vāṉat tavarku.   (*TKL* 86)

> Who entertains an "unknown person" and looks for the
> next one is a worthy "newcomer" to the Gods in heaven

(tr. Author)

This is a unique couplet wherein the unique cultural term *virundu* has been rendered thrice as follows: *celvirundu* (the outgoing unknown person entertained), *varuvirundu* (next unknown person to be entertained), and *nalvirundu* (worthy newcomer). In the first two instances, others are *the newcomers* whereas in the last, the host himself turns up as *a newcomer* to the Gods of heaven.

Entertaining/engaging *unknown people* who visit our homes is like conducting *vēḷvi* (Skt. *yajña*, the Vedic sacrificial fire). Its benefit cannot be measured by any scale than that of the standard and satisfaction of the entertained *virundu* (strangers), (*TKḶ* 87). The man of wealth is poor indeed if he fails to extend hospitality to unknown people (*TKḶ* 89). Such men are the losers destined not to reap the benefits of that *yajña* (*TKḶ* 88). However, a semantic mobility has taken place with the term *virundu* in modern times. We need to probe and understand the mobility of meaning from cultural aspects. The civilization and culture of Europeans, especially the British, soon after the 18th century, started greatly influencing Indians in all respects. Not only in dress-style-attitude but in every sphere, for instance in thought-speech-activities, Western culture slowly entered and effected a lot of significant changes. As a result, rapid industrialization took place at the cost of agriculture/farming. Innumerous schools were built up. The Macaulay Education System had, in fact, produced *literates* for clerical jobs in huge volume. Thereby, the nuclear family system has occurred at the cost of the traditional joint family system. Man started working and living more with machines than his kith and kin. In his machine-oriented lifestyle, there is no time and space for others except for his wife and children. It is more pathetic that in the prevailing global consumer world, even one's own parents become a burden to a man. So, there cropped up many 'old age homes' in cities and towns of India. In the present-day scenario, even a close relative has to inform about his/her visiting another's home well in advance. The European's highly sophisticated and individual-oriented way of life of *formal social culture*, no doubt, has made a great impact on and influenced hugely the Indian mind setup and their culture. The Tamils also have been incredibly influenced by such alien culture for the last few centuries. This is what seemed to have affected the real meaning of some age-old Tamil cultural terms like *nanri* (good action > thankfulness/gratitude/gratefulness), *virundu* (novelty/newness/ strangers > guests) at later days.

V

Nanri: Good Deed > Thankfulness/ Gratitude/Gratefulness

India, as an erstwhile British colony, has seen several changes/vicissitudes/incursions in every realm including languages, civilization and culture. Some cultural terms of Indian languages, in due course of time, have acquired new meanings as they encountered the British and their language and so have seen its influence on all spheres. So much so, some peculiar cultural terms of the Tamil language, which is known for its ancient civilization-cultural heritage, have seen significant changes in meaning. For instance, let us consider a unique Tamil term *nanri* and its actual meaning that prevailed in the past and its changed connotations in the present time.

The Tamil term *nanri,* which meant "good deed" in the past, is being rendered in the sense of *thankfulness, gratitude,* or *gratefulness* in the evolved modern Tamil, especially in written language. However, its original connotation was *naṟceyal*, 'good deed.' N. Kathiraiverpillai (1984: 870) gives its meaning as *upakāra guṇam*, (helping nature) and *naṉmai*, (goodness) English men used to acknowledge formally whatsoever good thing/help rendered by anyone to them, either by love or obligation, with the term 'thanks.' It is doubtful whether the term is always rendered consciously in the sense of gratitude. Though it is an expression of evolved civilization, it is habitually rendered in the sense of formality or customary behaviour. As we know, the whole European society, including the British, is built upon/centered on *formal relationship*. There exists a private space even between the biological parents and their own children. In their culture, a *formal relationship* is required and welcomed. Contrary to this Western culture, as we know, Indian society as a society based on *informal relationships* is built on a strong love equation. Typically, there exists no space among family members for the private sphere or formal customary behaviour in the psyche of Indians, including the Tamils, as the society is built on gapless, intense relationships over two millennia. Hence, our forefathers did not acknowledge someone's help or good act by merely uttering the word *naṉri* (thanks) until modern times. However, they conveyed their sense of "gratitude" by some or other "good action" (*naṉri*) in return. The actual meaning of the term *naṉri* was indeed *good deed* or *good action* in ancient times but certainly not in the connotation of *gratitude/thankfulness*, the prevailing meaning at present. Perhaps, there exists no exclusive word as such in any Indian language to convey the exact meaning of the English term thankfulness/gratefulness/gratitude.[24] When someone conveys his/her sense of gratitude for the help which he/she gets by the English term 'thanks,' it sounds quite natural, whereas the Tamil word *naṉṟi* obviously echoes unnatural or artificial sound bites.

The term *naṉṟi* has been rendered in the sense of *good deed* or *good act* alone in the Sangam poems and *Tirukkuṟaḷ*. A hero in *Kuṟuntogai* anthology[25] in the clandestine love phase contemplates going in search of wealth by leaving his beloved. Then the *tōḻi* (confidante) asks him to come early with the wealth earned to get married to her friend. She states,

> Lord of the huge mountains
> where an elephant calf suckles
> on her mother's abundant breasts!
> If you are not like the king
> on the throne who forgot gratitude (*naṉṟi*, 'good deed')
> to those who helped him in bad times,
> but remain constant in not
> forgetting the favors you got from us,
> the girl with thick, soft hair that of a
> delicate peacock, will be yours alone.
>
> (Kabilar, *Kuṟuntogai* 225, tr. Vaidehi Herbert,[26]
> the parenthesis is added by the author)

The author Vaidehi Herbert, in the above translation, has mistakenly rendered the term "gratitude" (appearing in the fifth line) for the Tamil word *naṉṟi,* which evidently means "good deed." The translator, by considering the prevailing meaning of the present day for the term *naṉṟi* of the bygone heroic age, has misinterpreted it as *gratitude* instead of *good deed*. It is to be noted here that as such the noun *gratitude*, the sense of gratefulness, cannot be forgotten. It is semantically erroneous. But any act, either good or bad, can be forgotten in due course of time. The *tōḻi* implicitly refers to *the sexual union* that has taken place sometime in the past between the hero and the heroine as *naṉṟi,* 'the good action' (done by the latter to the former). She emphasizes that the hero should not forget that *nanri*, that 'good deed' when he accomplishes his mission of earning wealth. And she reminds him to remember the *blissful union*, 'the good action' that he had had with the heroine some time ago. Subsequently, she urges him to come back to wed her without settling down on alien land by marrying someone else.

It may be stated here that exactly in the aforesaid connotation alone (good deed), the term *nanri* is rendered in all other Sangam anthologies too. However, some translators of classical anthologies like Vaidehi Herbert somehow failed to read the word's actual connotation and misinterpreted it almost in all places. For instance, let us consider the following *Narrinai* (*NRI*) poem 330. The hero in the poem maintains an extramarital relationship with some women of ill-reputation. Regrettably, he is also contemplating marrying them at some point in time and wishes to lead a family life by keeping them in the same house along with the heroine, his legitimate wife. In such a critical situation, the *tōḻi* makes him understand clearly that though he can marry them, he might not read what actually lies in their wicked minds; and it is even more unlikely his mistresses could become (*empāḍādal,* "becoming like us," so says the *tōḻi* rhetorically in an inclusive term) like his *nanri cānra* (well mannered) virtuous/chaste woman (wife) to bring forth boys along with girls wearing lovely bangles to him. Here we may comprehend the actual meaning from the stanzas of the Tamil poem given below:

> *yāṇar ūraniṉ māṇilai magaḷirai*
> *emmaṉait tandunī taḷīiyiṉum avartam*
> *puṉmaṉat tuṉmaiyō aridē avarum*
> *paintoḍi magaḷiroḍu ciṟuvarp payandu*
> *nanri cānra karpoḍu*

empā ḍādal adaṉiṉum aridē!

(Ālaṅkuḍi Vangaṉār, *Naṟṟiṇai* 330: 6–11)

Analyze the misapprehended translation of the above poem by Vaidehi Herbert[27] as follows:

> Even if you bring to our house your
> women with lovely jewels and embrace
> them, it is difficult to know what is in their
> minds, and it is even more difficult for
> them to bring forth girls with beautiful
> bracelets, and boys with gratitude and honor
> (to become like us, good mannered chaste women
> to bring forth boys along with girls
> wearing lovely bangles)

(tr. Vaidehi Herbert)
(The parenthesis with words in brackets
are added by the author)

The translator besides misreading the Tamil phrase *"naṉri cāṉra karpu"* by translating it as "with gratitude and honour" into English but also mistakenly adjoins the phrase with "girls with beautiful bracelets, and boys" instead of conjoining the same (well mannered) to the "chaste woman (wife)." Whatever may be the context the term *naṉri*—not only in the aforesaid poem but in the entire corpus of Sangam poems—needs to be rendered as *good deed* or simply as *good*, an adjective to any noun.

Contradicting her usual rendering of the Tamil term, *naṉri*, the translator Vaidehi Herbert, however, has equated it perfectly once into English as "good" to the stanza of a poem from the same *Naṟṟiṇai* anthology. Let us observe the Tamil stanzas of the poem:

> .... *vāntōy veṟpa!*
> *naṉri viḷaivum tīdoḍu varumeṉa*
> *aṉruṉar kaṟindaṉa ḷāyiṉ kuṉrattut*

tēmmudir cilambil taḍaiiya
vēymaruḷ paṇaittōḷ aḻiyalaḷ maṉṉē.

(Anonymous, *Naṟṟiṇai* 188: 5–9)

The hero frequently visits his ladylove during day times and clandestinely enjoys her love by the hillside. He has not thought of marrying his beloved and saving her reputation. As it becomes a worrisome matter, the heroine expects him to marry her at the earliest. Concerned for her esteemed life, the *tōḻi* refuses to arrange for the tryst anymore but urges him to marry her friend without any further delay. She makes it clear to him that the heroine will not allow him to exploit her physically anymore. So, she implicitly makes him understand the situation. The translator[28] here renders the Tamil term *naṉri* suitably as "good" and also puts the other details perfectly as in the following words:

> She understands well,
> that what can be good, can also lead to
> bad things. She will not let her curved,
> rounded arms, like bamboo, waste away
> in the mountain slopes with mature honey.

(tr. Vaidehi Herbert)

It may be mentioned here that the term *naṉri*[29] has been rendered exactly in the sense of "good deed" as in the couplets of *Tirukkuṟaḷ*. As we know, the ancient Tamil society, which highly regarded the agricultural profession, also duly respected the people engaged in academic activities, i.e., education. It, indeed, is considered as a *naṉri* (a good deed) of fathers—whosoever offers the best education possible to his son and makes him top in his school/institution. It is evident in the *Tirukkuṟaḷ* that follows:

tandai magaṟkāṟṟum naṉri avaiyattu
mundi iruppac ceyal.　　(*TKḺ* 67)

"The one good (*nanri*), which a father can give to his son, is to ensure the son is well educated and knowledgeable and is placed ahead of all those in the assembly of learned scholars" (Viswanathan, *Ibid.*, p. 25). When the translator R. Viswanathan renders the unique, culturally specific Tamil word *nanri* perfectly as "the one good" but his predecessors somehow could not catch up with the exact meaning as they have rendered it as "the benefit" (Drew & John Lazarus 1989: 15), as "duty" (Bharati 2008: 15) respectively. Here the Tamil phrase *tandai magarkārrum nanri* needs proper interpretation. If we consider the prevailing meaning of the phrase as thankfulness/gratitude/gratefulness, then we would end up with a gross mistake. Thereupon, the actual connotation of the term will become erroneous. Because no father needs to convey his *gratitude* (the present-day connotation of the word *nanri*) to his son but wants to do a *good deed* only. The learned men who excel in the fields of education-knowledge-wisdom-characteristics were indeed the need of the hour during the *Tirukkural* days as the man was gradually moving away from noble qualities. No doubt, it is only the knowledge acquired by education that provides ample scope for anyone to comprehend what is good or bad. Education, indeed, drives a man into a righteous path. Providing education is the one good deed that any father can do to his son even in ancient days. This is what seems to be the idea of Tiruvalluvar here. For the *nanri* (the good deed of providing a proper education) of (done by) the father, the son is expected to make sure of one thing that needs to be done in return. That is to make others say: "What great penance did his father to obtain him"! This is what Tiruvalluvar intends to connote by rendering the word *udavi*, 'the help' for denoting a befitting action in return that a son can do for his father.

magan tandaikkārrum udavi ivantandai
ennōrrān kollenuñ col.   (*TKL* 70)

The couplet delightfully states: "A son can render 'one help' to his father (for the good deed done by the latter) by making others express in amazement, "what penance did his father to obtain him!" A son is expected to ascend to that great position by his grand academic performance and role model characteristics. Essentially, the word *udavi* rendered in the couplet, in fact, draws our attention here. The great philosopher Tiruvalluvar has not employed any Tamil word meaning *duty* or *responsibility* in its place for denoting the *helping/supportive act* of the son. The author could have rendered the word *nanri* (in the present days' prevailing sense of thanks/gratitude/ gratefulness) instead of *udavi* here to indicate the *aiding* or *supportive act* of the son. But the preacher of "the Gospel of Maxims" has not done so, why? It is because **showing regard merely by words to any good deed of others is just a routine act that has no place in Tamil culture**. So, the son is expected to compensate for his father's good deed by his noble qualities by becoming learned.

Any action, either good or bad, does not suddenly show up with anyone. For any action, there are certain preceding factors and effects that crop up in future. Obviously, one's righteous conduct alone becomes the seed for his/her *nanri*, the *good action*. *Tīyolukkam*, the *bad actions* always bring troubles. This truth is impeccably delivered in the following *Tirukkural*.

nanrikku vittāgum nallolukkam tīyolukkam
enrum idumbait tarum.   (*TKL* 138)

Good conduct sows seeds of blessings
Bad conduct endless evil brings.

(tr. Bharati 2008: 29)

Though small in magnitude, "the *naṉri*, *'good action'* that is rendered at a crucial time is greater than the world" (*TKḶ* 102); "is bigger than the benefits of the ocean" (*TKḶ* 103). The knower of advantages weighs "the *naṉri* though it is as small as millet but as large as a palmyra tree" (*TKḶ* 104). Recognizing anybody's timely *good action* (*naṉri*) is termed as *ceynnaṉri aṟidal,* i.e., "remembering good deed (of others)." "If anyone forgets to think of someone's *good deed* rendered at crucial times, then there is no hope for him/her in the life to progress" (*TKḶ* 110), thus Tiruvaḷḷuvar pronounces emphatically in a couplet. Man normally tends to forget, especially, in matters not so gainful to him. While conveniently forgetting someone's good actions, he usually forgets the bad ones. What is it to be kept in mind and what is not to be? TVR clarifies the doubt in the following *Tirukkuṟaḷ.*

> *naṉri maṟappadu naṉraṉru naṉralladu*
> *aṉre maṟappadu naṉru.*   (*TKḶ* 108)

> It is not good to forget good deeds; good to forget
> bad deeds at that very moment.

> (tr. Author)

We can comprehend the meaning of the term *naṉri* rendered in the above couplet plainly as *good deed.* But if we consider the prevailing present connotation for the aforesaid term as *thankfulness/gratitude/gratefulness* then arises the ambiguity. What a person needs to remember is the *good deed* of others but not their *thankfulness* or *gratitude.* What a person needs to forget is the *bad deed* of others that too at the very moment. As there is no exclusive antonym for *naṉri* in Tamiḻ, Tiruvaḷḷuvar just adds *alladu*—(in the meaning of prefixes in English like *'ir/im/ in/un/non'* and so on)—*'a'* suffix in Tamiḻ denoting a negative sense to the existing term *naṉri* (*naṉru+alladu > naṉralladu* = "not good"). This indicates well the grand culture of the ancient Tamils as they did not conceive negative terms for certain positive words. For instance, the words *nanri* (good deed), and *nārram* (fragrance/good smell) as such do not have antonyms in Tamil. It is to be noted that the terms *nanri* and *nanru* are the synonyms rendered here for *good deed*. So, we do come across the word *nanru*[30] in the sense of the aforesaid term in several of *Tirukkural* couplets.

Therefore, it suffices to say that **honouring someone's *good deed* customarily by words was not a part of the ancient Tamils' culture** but certainly, a change has taken place in the connotation of the unique term *nanri* to mean *thankfulness/ gratitude/gratefulness* as well as in the Tamil culture soon after the advent of English education in our country.

VI

Nārram: Good Fragrance/Good Smell > Bad Smell/Rotten Smell

Indian culture, especially Tamil culture, before the advent of British, had significantly lost its identity with the invasion of Sanskrit culture. In the beginning, **the ancient Tamil society was not birth-based, caste-oriented hierarchical like the Aryan society.** As such, the hierarchal society was not then prevalent. Of course, ancient Tamil society had divisions based on profession yet arguably no hierarchy of high and low existed. Probably, the early Tamil society seems to have inherited Aryan's *Varṇāśrama Dharma*[31] during the *Tirukkural* period. In the place of now prevailing British/English culture, Aryan/Sanskrit culture was ruling over Tamil culture, till a few centuries ago. Notably, still we can see the supremacy of Sanskrit culture in the religious sphere such as temples, Gods, worship, festivals, rituals, and ceremonies. The irony is that nowadays, we see name plates hanging on the walls of temples of Tami<u>l</u> Nadu stating: *Ingut tami<u>l</u>ilum arccaṇai ceyyappaḍum* (*Arcana*[32] will be done here *also* in Tami<u>l</u>). The suffix *'um'* (*also*) added to the term "Tami<u>l</u>" is nothing but simply ridiculous. The temples are very much located on Tamil land, and the worshippers are also Tami<u>l</u>s. Besides, they are duly taken care of by the religious Tami<u>l</u>s and the Government of Tami<u>l</u> Nadu but strange is that Sanskrit only rules the Tami<u>l</u>s' religious sphere to date. **Regrettably, the most striking irony is that Tami<u>l</u> is scarcely seen even in the names of Tami<u>l</u>s, while Sanskrit is dominating for over a period of seventeen hundred years.**

It is a fact that there is a volume of differences between Sanskrit and Tami<u>l</u>, not only in the spheres of 'letters-words-meaning' but also in their 'theme-structure-style.' In the vocabulary of Sanskrit, like in any other language, there are plenty of positive terms that have negative parallels. As we know, positive terms in the English language become their negatives when some prefixes are added. For instance, the term 'possible' becomes negative as 'impossible' with the prefix *'im.'* Similarly, we could find such word formations in Sanskrit/Hindi too. There are many positive terms in Sanskrit that transform as negatives with the prefix *'a,'* the very first vowel letter of several languages including Sanskrit. For example, *nyāy* (justice) X *anyāy* (injustice); *nīti* (virtue/justice) X *anīti* (impropriety/injustice); *dharm* (righteousness) X *adharm* (immorality).

In a similar fashion, if a prefix *dur* (meaning in the sense of bad, wicked, devoid of) is added to some positive words then they lose their meanings and become negatives. For example, *adṛṣṭ* (luck/fortune) X *duradṛṣṭ* (unluck/misfortune); *ātmā* (soul) X *durātmā* (bad soul/spirit); *bhāgyā* (fortune) X *durbhāgyā* (misfortune). But there is no such word formation in the grammatical tradition of

Tamil. However, some Tamil positive terms with the aforesaid Sanskrit prefix *dur,* invariably become negative ones. Let us consider the Tamil term *nāṟṟam.* The term normally refers to *smell, scent, odour* (Vaiyapurippillai 1982: 2235) in a positive sense. But when it gets *dur,* a prefix of Sanskrit, then it means *bad smell, bad scent,* and *unpleasant odour*—all in the negative sense. Apparently, the term in the negative sense is very much in vogue for centuries in colloquial Tamils. Evidently, Sanskrit, the language of elites, has been ruling the minds of Tamil public, perhaps unconsciously, in the realm of language and vocabulary. The term commonly denoting smell/scent/odour, however, has been generally rendered in the poems of Sangam works and *Tirukkuṟaḷ* couplets, especially in the sense of (*good*) *smell, scent,* and *odour.* Before seeing some stanzas wherein the term occurs, let us know its etymological references with the following quotes.

Paripāḍal, the fifth book of the Eight Anthologies, comprises a number of theme poems on Vaiyai, the river of Madurai city, Lord Tirumāl (Vishnu) and Lord Murugan. Every religious person believes that his/her God is omnipotent and, resides eternally in each and everything. So, Vaishnavites do consider that their God Vishnu is ever dwelling omnipotent in the five basic elements of Nature. With such notions at his heart, a poet named Kaḍuvan Iḷaveyinanār, while rendering an invocation on Tirumāl, has employed the aforesaid term *nāṟṟam* in the following manner:

> *tīyinuḷ teralnī! pūvinuḷ nāṟṟamnī!*
> *kalliṉuḷ maṇiyumnī! colliṉuḷ vāymainī!*
> *aṟattiṉuḷ aṉbunī! maṟattiṉuḷ maindunī!*
> *vēdattu maṟainī! bhūdattu mudalumnī!*
> *veñcuḍar oḷiyumnī! tingaḷuḷ aḷiyumnī!*
> *aṉaittumnī! aṉaittiṉuḷ poruḷumnī! .....*

(Kaḍuvan Iḷaveyinanār, *Paripāḍal* 3: 63–68)

> You are the heat within the fire; Fragrance within the flower;
> Gem within the stone; Truth within the word;
> Mercy within justice; Might behind valour;
> Secret within the scripture; Foremost among elements;
> Splendour in the sun; Coolness in the moon;
> You are everything; and also the inner substance of these.
>
> (tr. Pandiyan)[33]

Unambiguously the meaning of the term *nāṟṟam*, occurring in the abovementioned poem, is very clear. The poet while expressing every splendid attribute of Lord Vishṇu, sees Him as the *nāṟṟam* of flowers too. As flowers are mostly known for their *captivating fragrance* and *delightful luster*, also some other poets of *Paripāḍal* perceive the Lord in the same vein. Thus, the term has occurred in a few more poems in *Paripāḍal* as follows:

> *niṉ nāṟṟamum oṇmaiyum pūvaiyuḷa*
>
> (Kaḍuvaṉ Iḷaveyiṉaṉār, *Paripāḍal* 4: 29)
>
> Your fragrance and luster are in the
> *kāyā* flowers!
>
> (tr. Vaidehi Herbert)[34]
>
> *pulamum pūvaṉum nāṟṟamumnī*
>
> (Unknown, *Paripāḍal* 1: 48–49)
>
> You are the Vedas, the Brahma and fragrance.
>
> (tr. Author)

Etymologically, the term *nāṟṟam* is derived from the verbal root *nāṟu* and the suffix '*am*,' a metrical syllable making verbs as nouns in Tamiḻ. The root word *nāṟu* simply means to emit a sweet smell, to give forth perfume (Vaiyapurippillai,

Ibid., p. 2236) and to release a good fragrance. Since God is perceived as the eternal grace and the shining light, the poets often earnestly see Him as a flower that emits good smell; and extends the delightful luster. Contrary to this connotation, the same term *nāṟu* is very rarely rendered denoting *bad smell* or *stench/stink* in some poems while linked to the term *pulavu* (flesh). As an infinitive, the term *pulavu* simply means "to smell (of) raw flesh" (*Ibid.*, p. 2787) or "raw fish." For example, a poet named *Iḷavēṭṭaṉār* in *Ahanāṉūṟu* anthology employs this term exactly in the aforesaid connotation. He refers to a big-trunked elephant that attacked a huge tiger in a wild forest through which a hero goes regularly at night to see his beloved. In the big fight, the tiger gets defeated. Its blood and flesh got sprinkled over the elephant's trunk in the struggle. They began smelling bad. Aptly referring to this stinking smell, the poet employs the phrase *pulavunāṟu* in the second stanza of the poem following:

> *irumpuli tolaitta peruṅkai vēḻattup*
> *pulavunāṟu pugarnudal kaḻuvak kangul*
> *aruvi tanda aṇaṅguḍai neḍuṅkōṭṭu*

(Madurai Aruvai Vāṇigaṉ Iḷavēṭṭaṉār, *Ahanāṉūṟu* 272: 1–3)

But in the same poem, its own noun form *nāṟṟam* is strikingly rendered in the positive connotation, viz. *fragrance/good smell*. The hero is depicted as seeing his ladylove regularly at the usual meeting spot of 'night-tryst' (*iravukkuṟi*). One night, when he is about to reach the spot, his beloved is expressing her worry to her *tōḻi*, about whether he will marry her soon or not. Thereafter the confidante (as the nearby lover listens) shares her positive opinion with her that he will marry her soon. In her conversation, she mentions his attire adorned with flowers. She says then that the hero wearing a strand of *kūdaḷam* flowers woven with wild jasmine (that grow abundantly near flowing water) were just spreading their *nārram*s (fragrances) pleasantly. From the above sketch, we can understand that Tamiḻ men in the past did wear flowers like their women but in the forms of *kaṇṇi* (a cluster of flowers tied on either side of the string) and *tār* (one end untied garland of flowers) that project them good-looking and sweet-smelling by the sheer luster and fragrance of flowers. This cultural fact is mentioned in *Kalittogai* (*KLT*), (the sixth book of Eight Anthology) as well, in the following words:

> *nīrnīvik kañaṉrapūk kamaḷuṅkāl niṉmārbiṉ*
> *tārnārram eṉayivaḷ madikkumaṉ madittāṅgē*
>
> (Nallanduvaṉār, *Kalittogai* 126: 10–11)
>
> When she smells the fragrant blossoms in the water,
> she'll think they are from your garlanded chest.
>
> (tr. Vaidehi Herbert)[35]

The phrase *tārnārram*, appearing in the second line of the quoted poem, conspicuously expresses that the (one end) untied garland worn by the hero was fragrant like the sweet-smelling flowers that blossom in the pools of the seashore. Not only these water bodies but also other native water sources like *kuḷam* (ponds), and *poygai* (natural/full ponds) naturally tend to emit a good smell as they are hugely filled with a variety of flowers, and creepers like *vaḷḷai*. For instance, the phrase *nārramcāl naḷipoygai* (cool pond filled with 'the great fragrance' of flowers) as mentioned in one of the poems of *Kalittogai* (16: 11) evidently reveals the aforesaid fact.

In earlier days, weddings of Tamiḻs traditionally took place before sunrise. The same ancient family/social functions nowadays take place after sunrise but before noon. As a variety of fragrant flowers are available abundantly in Tamiḻ Nadu, Tamiḻs are known for bedecking brides and bridegrooms and lavishly decorating the wedding halls. The couple and marriage halls thus beautified with fragrant flowers stupendously produce captivating, sweet-smells all around, especially in the cool, early morning hours. To depict this fact, a poet named Marudaṇiḻa Nāgaṇār has rendered it so poetically while describing the extramarital relationship of a hero in a poem (*KLT* 66: 9–12). The hero returns home with a lovely fragrance at dawn after seeking sexual pleasure with women adorned with flowers. As he had the blissful meeting with other women, having decked himself with sweet-smelling flowers, his body was still emitting the splendid fragrance in the early hours. The heroine points out his infidelity, though sarcastically but aesthetically, with the fine words *vaduvai yaṅkamaḻ nārram vaigaraip perradai (Ibid.).*[36] It is noticeable that the term *nārram*, as worded in this sentence, just denotes *good fragrance/sweet smell.* Exactly, in the same sense, the term has been rendered by several Sangam poets.[37]

Later, just in the same connotation of *good fragrance/sweet smell*, the term *nārram* has occurred in *Tirukkuraḷ* also in two couplets. A hero after meeting his beloved, exchanges his views about the beauty of her physical features with his close friend. He praises,

> *murimēṇi muttam muruval verinārram*
> *vēluṇkaṇ vēyttōḷ avaṭku.*   (*TKḶ* 1113)

> The bamboo-shouldered has pearl-like smiles,
> Fragrant breath and lance-like eyes.

> (tr. Bharati 2008: 229)

The hero feels that his beloved's natural body smell is an *intoxicating fragrance (verinārram).* Similarly, another hero shares his feelings about the smile of his sweetheart with the *tōḻi* and eulogizes:

> *mugaimokkuḷ uḷḷadu nāṟṟampōl pēdai*
> *nagaimokkuḷ uḷḷadoṉ ṟuṇḍu.*   (*TKḺ* 1274)

> Like scent in bud secrets conceal
> In the bosom of her half smile.

(tr. Bharati 2008: 261)

He assumes and conveys to the confidante that there is something concealed already in the heroine's meek smile like *the fragrance* (*nāṟṟam*) is contained in yet to be blossomed bud.

As we have seen, the term *nāṟṟam* thus referring to *sweet smell* denoted only such meanings in Tamiḻ literary works until the modern period. We are unable to trace when such a change has taken place in its positive meaning, and in what context. It needs to be mentioned here that the very positive term does have no negative word in Tamiḻ, neither in colloquial nor in written language to date, except the Sanskritized term *durnāṟṟam*. It is a unique culture of Tamiḻs—certain inauspicious events/ incidents/things are not to be mentioned openly but referred to with some auspicious terms. The very word underlines the fact that sometimes some words of some languages could lose their original meanings and earn new implications when they encounter other languages and their cultural elements.

While these terms *cāṉṟōr* (noble men), *naṉṟi* (good deed), *naṭpu* (love, i.e., sexual relationship), *nōkku* (sight of love), *virundu* (novelty), and *nāṟṟam* (fragrance) on the one hand act as a tool to grasp the literary heritage of Tamiḻ language, on the other, they serve as historical evidence to understand the cultural haritage as well as cultural mobility of Tamiḻs. Though not always explicitly, otherwise these terms do convey the encounters that took place between Tami<u>l</u>s and Aryans on one hand and British on the other at different times. In a nutshell, behind the formation and changes of meaning that took place with some words, often, there are various socio-religious-cultural factors that act as bolts and nuts.

Notes

*   This essay is the revised version of the paper titled "Deciphering the Peculiar Cultural Significance of Some Terms in Tirukku<u>r</u>a<u>l</u>," presented in the 9th *International Conference-Seminar on Tami<u>l</u> Studies,* held at University of Malaya, Kuala Lumpur, Malaysia, during 29th Jan.–01st Feb. 2015.

1.   *Cā<u>nr</u>ā<u>n</u>mai* (sublimity/virtue/goodness): *TK<u>L</u>* 981, 989, 990.

2.   *Cālbu* (excellence, nobility, greatness etc.): *TK<u>L</u>* 983, 984, 986–988, 1013, 1064.

3.   *Mā<u>t</u>ciyi<u>r</u> periyōr* (the great personae of glorious traits): Ka<u>n</u>iya<u>n</u> Pū<u>n</u>ku<u>nr</u>a<u>n</u>ār, *Pu<u>r</u>anā<u>n</u>ū<u>r</u>u* 192: 11–12.

4.   *ī<u>nr</u>u pu<u>r</u>antarudal e<u>n</u>talaik kaḍa<u>n</u>ē*
     cā<u>nr</u>ō<u>n</u> ākkudal tandaikkuk kaḍa<u>n</u>ē
     vēlvaḍittuk koḍuttal kollarkuk kaḍa<u>n</u>ē
     na<u>nn</u>aḍai nalgal vēndarkuk kaḍa<u>n</u>ē
     o<u>l</u>iruvā<u>l</u> aruñcamam murukkik
     ka<u>l</u>i<u>r</u>erindu peyardal kā<u>l</u>aikkuk kaḍa<u>n</u>ē.

     (Po<u>n</u>muḍiyār, *Pu<u>r</u>anā<u>n</u>ū<u>r</u>u* 312)

5.   *ci<u>rr</u>il na<u>rr</u>ū<u>n</u> pa<u>rr</u>i ni<u>n</u>maga<u>n</u>*
     yāṇḍu<u>l</u>a <u>n</u>ōve<u>n</u>a vi<u>n</u>avudi e<u>n</u>maga<u>n</u>
     yāṇḍu<u>l</u>a <u>n</u>āyi<u>n</u>um a<u>r</u>iyē<u>n</u> ōrum
     pulicērndu pōgiya kalla<u>l</u>ai pōla
     ī<u>nr</u>a vayi<u>r</u>ō iduvē
     tō<u>nr</u>uva<u>n</u> mādō pō<u>r</u>kka<u>l</u>at tā<u>n</u>ē

     (Kāva<u>r</u>peṇḍu, *Pu<u>r</u>anā<u>n</u>ū<u>r</u>u* 86)

6. *yāṇḍupala vāga naraiyila āgudal*
    yāngāgiya reṉa viṉavudir āyiṉ
    māṇḍayeṉ maṉaiviyoḍu makkaḷum nirambiṉar;
    yāngaṉ ḍaṉaiyareṉ iḷaiyarum; vēndaṉum
    allavai ceyyāṉ ākkum adantalai
    āṉravin daḍangiya koḷgaic
    cāṉrōr palaryāṉ vāḷum ūrē.

    (Picirāndaiyār, *Puṟanāṉūṟu* 191)

7. Source: http://sangamtranslationsbyvaidehi.com/purananuru-151-200/

8. *īṉra poḷudiṟ periduvakkum taṉmagaṉaic*
    cāṉrōṉ eṉakkēṭṭa tāy   (*TKḶ* 69)

9. *Cāṉrōr: TKḶ* 115, 118, 148, 197, 299, 328, 458, 656-57, 802, 840,
    922, 923, 982, 985, 1014, 1078.

10. *Cāṉrōr: Nālaḍiyār* 68, 100, 126, 133, 151-153, 165, 179, 190, 227,
    298, 316, 343-44, 349, 356-57, 368.

11. *Kaṇṇiṉai nōkku* (the sight of love of two eyes): *TKḶ* 1100;
    ciṟunōkkam (glance/gaze): *TKḶ* 1092; *nōkka* (to glance/gaze/look):
    TKḶ 1098; *nōkkam* (glancing/gazing): *TKḶ* 1085; *nōkkāmai* (not
    glancing/gazing): *TKḶ* 1095; *nōkki* (having glanced/gazed): *TKḶ*
    1173, 1093, 1279; *nōkkiya* (glanced/gazed): *TKḶ* 1172; *nōkkināḷ* (she
    who glanced/gazed): *TKḶ* 1082, 1093; *nōkkiṉum* (even if glanced/
    gazed): *TKḶ* 1320; *nōkku* (sight of love/glance/gaze): *TKḶ* 972,
    1082, 1091, 1094, 1097; *nōkkudal* (glancing/gazing): *TKḶ* 1099;
    edirnōkku (counter glance/gaze): *TKḶ* 1082; *piṟaṉ maṉai nōkkāda*
    pērāṇmai (noble manliness of not glancing/gazing/looking at the
    wife of others): *TKḶ* 148; *podu nōkku* (common looking): *TKḶ*
    1099; *maḍa nōkku* (the meek looks of hind or fawn like looks/gaze/
    glance): *TKḶ* 1089; *nilaṉ nōkkum* (stoop looking/glancing/gazing at
    the ground): *TKḶ* 1114.

12. Source: http://sangamtranslationsbyvaidehi.com/akananuru-301-400/

13. Source: http://sangamtranslationsbyvaidehi.wordpress.com/kuruntho-
        kai-1-100/

14. *māṉpiṉai nōkkiṉ maḍanal lāḷai*
    īṉra naṭpiṟ karuḷā ṉāyiṉum

(Kayamaṉār, *Ahanāṉūṟu* 195)

uyirkalan doṉṟiya doṉrupaḍu naṭpiṟ
ceyirtīr neñcamoḍu cerindōr pōla
ārtuyil iyambu nāḍaṉ

(Nakkīrar, *Ahanāṉūṟu* 205)

mārpurit tāgiya maṟuvil naṭpē

(Cēndam Bhūdaṉār, *Ahanāṉūṟu* 247)

peruvarai aḍukkattuk kiḻavōṉ eṉṟum
aṉṟai yaṉṉa naṭpiṉaṉ

(Kabilar, *Kuṟnutogai* 385)

Source: http://sangamtranslationsbyvaidehi.com/akananuru-301-400/

17. *māṉpiṉai nōkkiṉ maḍanal lāḷai*
    īṉṟa naṭpiṟ karuḷā ṉāyiṉum

    (Kayamaṉār, *Ahanāṉūṟu* 195)

18. *Naṭpu* (everlasting emotional/soul mingled relationship): *TKḶ* 106, 107, 187, 338, 381, 781-82, 785-91, 793-95, 798, 800-03, 813, 816-17, 821, 829-30, 874, 1122, 1165.

19. *Keḻutagamai* (friendship): *TKḶ* 700, 802-04, 808.

20. *Kēṇmai* (friendship): *TKḶ* 106, 441, 519, 709, 782, 792, 797-98, 800, 807, 809, 811-12, 815, 822, 838.

21. *Toḍarbu* (friendship): *TKḶ* 783, 802, 806, 819-20, 920.

22. *Naṭṭār* (friends): *TKḶ* 192, 679, 804-05, 808, 826, 908, 1293.

23. *Virundu* (new people/unknown people/strangers): *TKḶ* 43, 81-90, 153, 1211, 1268.

24. For instance, let us infer etymologically the meanings of the following Hindi terms: *shukriya* (*shu* > *su* = excellent, + *kriya* = action > lit. excellent action; *shubh* = auspicious/benign + *kriya* = action/deed > *shubhkriya* > *shukriya* > lit. auspicious/benign action; *su* = pious/good, + *karm* = action/deed > *sukarm* > lit. pious/good action).

25. *kanrutan payamulai mānda munril*
    tinaipiḍi unnum peruṅkal nāḍa!
    keṭṭaviḍat tuvanda udavi kaṭṭil
    vīruperru maranda mannan pōla
    nanrimaran damaiyā yāyin mencīrk
    kalimayir kalāvattanna ivaḷ
    olimen kūndal uriyavāl ninakkē!

    (Kabilar, *Kuruntogai* 225)

26. Source: http://sangamtranslationsbyvaidehi.com/kurunthokai-201-300/

27. Source: http://sangamtranslationsbyvaidehi.com/natrinai-301-400/

28. Source: http://sangamtranslationsbyvaidehi.com/natrinai-101-200/

29. *Nānri* (good deed): *TKḶ* 67, 97, 102, 104, 108, 110, 138, 685, 994;
    Nānrikkan: TKḶ 117; *Nānri payavā vinai: TKḶ* 439, 652; *Ceynnānri:*
    TKḶ 110.

30. *Nānru* (good deed): *TKḶ* 108-09, 422, 467, 715, 932, 1072, 1225.

31. *Varṇāśrama Dharma: Varṇā* means colour and historians tell us
    that the fair-skinned Aryans (migrating from Iran and Asia Minor)
    found the indigenous people in the Indus Valley region dark. From
    this gradually evolved the caste system, which regulated interaction
    and intercourse among the Aryan and non-Aryan people of India.
    This system came to be called *chaturvarṇa* (four colours) because
    it identified four stratas of people in society. (*cf.*: C.T. Indira, *The*
    legend of Nandan – Nandan Kathai, p. xvi)

32. *Arcana* is a Sanskrit term denotes a form of worship performed
    in temples/shrines offering flowers, fruits, coconut, while reciting
    Sanskrit *sloka*s and *mantra*s as per Vedic practice.

33. Source: http://en.wikipedia.org/wiki/Paripāṭal

34. Source: http://sangamtranslationsbyvaidehi.com/kali-pal/

35. Source: http://sangamtranslationsbyvaidehi.com/a-kalithokai-neythal/

36. *anaimentōḷ yāmvāḍa amartunai puṇarndunī*
    manamanaiyā yenavanda mallalin mānbanrō
    podukkoṇda kavvaiyil pūvanip polindanin
    vaduvaiyan kamalnārram vaigaraip perradai

    (Marudaṇiḷa Nāgaṇār, *Kalittogai* 66: 9–12)

I, with my soft, delicate arms am fading away, and you
have been in pleasurable pursuits with women you
desire, in their homes. Causing slander, you united with
women adorned with flowers. You have come here at
dawn with their lovely fragrances, for me to see your splendor.

(tr. Vaidehi Herbert)

Source: http://sangamtranslationsbyvaidehi.com/a-kalithokai-
marutham/

37. *orūu koḍiyiyal nallār kuralnāṟṟat tuṟṟa*
muḍiyudir pūntādu moymbiṉa vāgat
toḍiya yemakkunī yāraiyō periyārkku
aḍiyarō yāṟṟādavar

(Marudaniḷa Nāgaṉār, *Kalittogai* 88: 1–4)

Go away! Who are you to touch me, coming
here with pollen dropped from the flowers
adorning the thick, fragrant hair of vine-like
concubines? Is the one who is suffering any
inferior to the one who is powerful?

(tr. Vaidehi Herbert)

Source: http://sangamtranslationsbyvaidehi.com/a-kalithokai-
marutham/

veṟikamaḻ koṇda nāṟṟamum ciṟiya
pacalai pāytaru nudalum nōkki
vaṟidugu neñcinaḷ piṟidoṉru kāṭṭi
veyya yuyirttanaḷ yāyē

(Kabilar, *Naṟṟiṇai* 368: 6–9)

Smelling the strong fragrance in her
thick dark hair, and looking at the pallor
on her small forehead, mother sighed deeply.

(tr. Vaidehi Herbert)

Source: http://sangamtranslationsbyvaidehi.com/natrinai-301-400/

koḍiyayai vāḻi tumbi innōy
paḍugadil amma yāṉiṉak kuraitteṉa

....

tāṟupaḍu pīram ūdi vēṟupaḍa
nāṟṟa miṉmaiyiṟ pacalai ūdāy

(Tumbicēr Kīraṉīr, *Naṟṟiṇai* 277: 1–8)

O cruel honeybee! May you live long!
You swarm clusters of *peerkai*
flowers on the thorn fence
protecting our house, and do not
buzz around my fragrance-lacking
body with yellow pallor spots.
I am afflicted with pain.

(tr. Vaidehi Herbert)

Source: http://sangamtranslationsbyvaidehi.com/natrinai-201-300/

pulavunāṟ ṟatta paintaḍi
pūnāṟ ṟatta pugaikoḷīi ūṉcuvai
kaṟicō ṟuṇḍu varundutoḻi lalladu
piṟidutoḻi laṟiyā vāgaliṉ naṉṟum

(Kabilar, *Puṟanāṉūṟu* 14: 12–15)

The hands of those who sing your praises, are soft since they know
no stress, other than that of eating rice cooked with meat, and
chunks of fresh meat roasted in fire with flower-fragrant smoke.

(tr. Vaidehi Herbert)

Source: http://sangamtranslationsbyvaidehi.com/purananuru-1-50/

nāṟṟa uṇavi ṉoru māṟṟa
arumpeṟa lulagam niṟaiya
virundupeṟ ṟaṉarāl poliganum pugaḻē!

(Kaḻāttalaiyār, *Puṟanāṉūṟu* 62: 17–19)

Those who eat fragrant food, wear flowers that don't fade, do
not blink, and guide the new arrivals in the other world that
is so hard to obtain. May the glory of both of you glow!

(tr. Vaidehi Herbert)

Source: http://sangamtranslationsbyvaidehi.com/purananuru-51-100/

*tuṉiyal malaruṇkaṉ colvēṟu nāṟṟam
kaṉiyiṉ malariṉ mayirkaṟ cīppiṉṉadu
tuṉiyal naṉinīniṉ cūḷ*

(Nallanduvaṉār, *Paripāḍal* 8: 53–55)

One with flower-like eyes! Do not
be angry. What you say is not right. The odor is
that of fruits and flowers carried by the wind.
I swear   ……   ……   ……

(tr. Vaidehi Herbert)

Source: http://sangamtranslationsbyvaidehi. com/kali-pal/

*tōṟṟamō rotta malarkamaḻ taṉcāndiṉ
nāṟṟattiṟ pōṟṟi nagaiyoḍum pōttandu*

(Nallaḻiciyār, *Paripāḍal* 16: 25–26)

He sees her
looks like that of a flower, is aware of the cool fragrance
of sandal, laughs and leaves with her.

(tr. Vaidehi Herbert)

Source: http://sangamtranslationsbyvaidehi.com/kali-pal/

Chapter: Three

From Sleeping to Salvation: Vedic Codes and Practices*

Every society, since anthropological times or at least from the pre-historical period, has been built upon or governed by certain faiths/religions, ceremonies/rituals, customs/social norms, rules and regulations/laws, and so on. Arts and literature that emerge from any given socio-religious-cultural milieu naturally have a greater role in evolving and establishing people's cultural traits. As stated earlier in the previous chapter, every literary work, irrespective of its genre, has to have the twofold functions, viz. 'educate' and 'entertain' people. In this endeavour, didactic works primarily aim to 'educate' or 'impart' certain ideas, viewpoints, thoughts, values, or philosophies, rather than 'entertaining.' In contrast, other literary genres—such as lyrics, epics, novels, short stories, and plays—primarily focus on 'entertainment,' although they may have also 'educate' or 'convey' certain life values to some extent. Educating people is a kind of masculine act typically carried out since ages by the authoritative feudal lords, hegemonic bourgeois, highly learned, of course eloquent poets. Virtues, nobilities, duties, responsibilities, seldom rights are usually imparted to people while educating them. Obviously, every religion brainwashes people to

uphold certain virtues, to undergo varied kinds of *vrat*s (obser-
vances/fasts) and perform some specific rituals in the disguise of
religious observance.

Conspicuously, we notice the influence of different religions in the thoughts and cultural life of Tamiḻs—the people
of pre-historic ethnicity who possess a long heritage of socio-
political-religious and philosophical merits like the esteemed
Greeks. Especially, we see the influences of canons, doctrines,
and ideologies of Jainism, Buddhism and Vedic Hinduism
seemingly in the corpus of eighteen Tamiḻ Didactic works
called "Padiṉeṉ Kīḻkkaṇakku Nūlgaḷ"[1] (*c.* 250–600 CE). The
manner these entities of faiths entering the religious systems
and social norms of the ancient Tamiḻs—is indeed a phenome-
non which warrants an earnest study. As we are aware, among
the three creeds mentioned above, only Vedic Hinduism is constantly prevailing in the realm of Indian culture by becoming
hand in gloves—shrewdly managing strong nexus with the entities of ruling classes and feudal societies. The orthodox codes
and practices of Brāhmaṇism protected and pronounced for
centuries by *rishi*s (sages), *sādhu*s (saints), kings, and *ācārya*s
(preceptors)/*guru*s (spiritual teachers/guides/masters/mentors)
are conspicuously seen in *Ācārakkōvai*[2] ('The Garland of Right
Conducts'), a prominent didactic work comprising 100 *veṇpās*[3]
(one of the four major metres of Tamiḻ prosody), composed by
Kayattūr Peruvāyiṉ Muḷḷiyār. This is a peculiar Tamiḻ ethical work that contains evidence of being largely influenced by
Sanskrit's literary works, viz. Vedas and *Dharmaśāstra*s. The
various instructions prescribed in the text are for personal rituals and accurate methods that every individual needs to follow.
The present essay attempts to analyze the backdrops, merits
and demerits of the Vedic codes and practices put forth by the
aforesaid versifier.

Valour and Virtue: The Unique Attributes of Ancient Tamiḻs

We understand history, civilization and culture of ancient Tamiḻs—the earliest ethnicity like the Greeks of pre-Heroic age—through *Tolkāppiyam* (*c.* 300 BCE), the earliest Tamiḻ grammatical text, and *Eṭṭuttogai* and *Pattuppāṭṭu* called "Sangam Literature" (*c.* 200 BCE–200 CE). In the poems of bygone era, the literatures of *aham*[4] and *puṟam*[5] themes were equally represented and respected. The manner the love feelings (*aham,* "interior feelings") of women are depicted in high regard, the non-love feelings and valiant behaviours (*puṟam*, "exterior actions") of men such as valour, dignity, warfare skill and other characteristics like munificence, mourning, etc., are also held in high esteem in ancient time. During the monarchal period that followed the age of clan/ tribal society, the ruling power solely rested with chieftains/ kings. The rulers then were hugely attracted and fascinated towards land, wealth and women. So, there were countless battles/wars frequently among the great Tamiḻ monarchs, viz. Cēra, Cōḻa and Pāṇḍiya, and several chieftains due to the undue interest and importance shown towards the aforesaid three attractions. Due to the frequent invasions, battles/wars, plentiful lands became barren, numerous thriving cities and forts became devastated beyond repairing, countless bountiful water resources turned tightfisted, abundant wealth got looted, beautiful women held abducted and abused, defeated kings and their subjects ended as slaves. Adverse attributes such as self-centeredness, egoism, arrogance, prowling, and what not, indeed made kings and chieftains turn oppressors/tyrants/ dictators. These rulers quite often caused grave injustice to the subjects of their opponents and at times their own people as well. Hence, prodigious poets valuing high every human being's welfare had rendered a volley of poems then in the quest to correct the erring rulers. The sovereigns by and large paid heed to their advice, at times even to their reprimands. However, there is no tangible or notable progress in the realm of ruling. Having become fatigued of habitually invading their opponents now and then, the emperors hailed from the great three Tamiḻ dynasties, viz. Cēra, Cōḻa and Pāṇḍiya, started losing their high esteem and became weakened by the end of 300 CE. Kalabhras, originally a dynasty belonging to Andhra Pradesh who entered Tamiḻ Nadu through Karnataka, had shrewdly exploited the deplorable socio-political situation to their benefit. These kings, staunch followers of Jainism, who entered Tamiḻ Nadu through Karnataka had ruled the country nearly for three hundred years, i.e., from *c.* 300–600 CE. Well before their advent, Aryans had already entered the Dravidian land and established their stronghold over Tamiḻs. The impact of the Aryan's Vedic religion was tangible on Tamiḻs to some extent, however not domineering or overriding the religious sentiment of the latter.

During the reign of the three great Tamiḻ emperors, *naḍukal valipāḍu* (the worship of an erected stone)—a distinctive tradition of the ancient Tamiḻ heroic culture—was widely practiced and held in high esteem. It honoured valiant heroes who became martyrs while bravely fighting in battles or wars. Worshipping the gods/goddesses of 'Great Tradition' did not have its footprint profoundly at that time. Deities were schemed as a constituent in the subjects of the fourteen background elements or native elements called *karupporuḷgaḷ* as depicted in the Sangam *aham* poems. There was no notion of the "Creator–Created" existed then. Hence, no nexus was found between the God and Tamiḻ humanity in the realm of religious faith. As no powerful Tami<u>l</u> king existed then to protect the legacy of Tami<u>l</u>s in the bleak situation of the post-Sangam period, the Tami<u>l</u>s witnessed recession and apparently suffered in all respects. Even mere existing traditionally became a colossal challenge to the people. Subsequently, their culture, arts and literature, philosophy, values, etc., have seen black out. The tenets and ceremonies of Jainism and Buddhism backed by the rulers, the Vedic codes and practices propped by higher communities were vehemently forced upon the common people. Consequently, the attributes held in high regard in the 'Heroic Age' (*c.* 3000 BCE–300 CE) such as valour, honour/dignity, munificence, etc., have been scantly regarded. The doctrines of Jainism, Buddhism, and Vedic Hinduism—promoted by rulers and influential elites—were presented as virtues, duties and responsibilities to be upheld by the common people. However, these ethical systems often appear to have been mechanisms through which the upper castes sought to reinforce their dominance and control over others. In caste-ridden India, particularly in the context of Tami<u>l</u> Nadu, the upper classes historically included kings, ministers, priests, *brāhmiṇs*, *veḷḷāḷas*, *mudaliyārs*, *vaishyas*, learned men, poets and others of high social standing. Conversely, socially and economically marginalized communities—such as *vēḍar* (hunters), *pāṇar* (minstrels), *paḷḷar* (bonded labourers attached to farmland), *paṟaiyar* (drummers), *pulaiyar* (scavengers), *paradavar* (fishermen), women and others—became the subjects of systematic subjugation. Although virtues, ethics, and duties were ostensibly intended for all, in practice they were disproportionately imposed upon and used to regulate the lives of these oppressed communities. In ancient society, rules and regulations were not equally executed for everyone. For instance, before the advent of British—the kings, priests, and *brāhmiṇs* were partially or totally exempted from paying land and house taxes. Also, these communities did enjoy some immunity from rigorous punishments even for their vigorous crimes.

All through history, the endorsement of the so-called *virtues* or *ethics*, is, in fact, nothing but the candid injunctions protecting the interest of feudal system thereby suppressing the interests of marginalized communities or disregarded classes. Since ages they are prevailing as sanctions rendered by dominants onto their underlings. The virtues/ethics are not just rulings/diktats. These decrees, in fact, have been playing a vital role in establishing the 'superb social regulations' profoundly as 'the perfect societal rulings' meant wholly for public wherein the hierarchal positions (top versus bottom) of privileged and underprivileged are tactfully justified and legitimized. Ethics shrewdly do validate the age-old social setup by claiming that the existing system is good for everyone. While diplomatically putting forth the views strongly for maintaining the *status quo,* they discreetly resist any sort of unrest among the people affected. In due course of time, the ethics of elitists become standardized and institutionalized. Thus, the moral codes accomplish the protection by stating them as natural laws, virtuous codes for each and everybody. The powerful dominant society punishes its people, particularly the weaker sections, by branding them as 'eccentricities,' 'mentally disordered,' and 'potential threats to the benevolent society' if they cross the line of moral codes endorsed by them. "In the history of mankind, it is mostly the marginalized folks who are being subjected to several kinds of physical punishments and mental tortures for centuries" (Raj Gauthaman 1997: 7). This is a kind of interpretation attributed to the so-called *virtues/ethics* (moral codes-duties-rights) authorized by society's prevailing class.

Ethical Codes and Practices in
'Inner' and 'Outer Spheres'

Any society is essentially built upon certain binary oppositions, viz. lord *vs.* slave, master *vs.* servant, bourgeoise *vs.* proletariat, higher *vs.* lower, noble *vs.* ignoble, learned *vs.* unlearned, and so on. Here we could perceive that the entities placed on the left side and right side respectively denote definite virtuous and wicked properties. Nonetheless, not one and all might accept and respect the existence of such properties as just right. We could understand the reason behind the rejection because these binary oppositions are being endorsed from the standpoint of traditionalists who emphasize all sorts of ethics to society. It is obvious that the folks subjected to oppression for ages would naturally have a different viewpoint in this regard. *Tirukkuṟaḷ* too very clearly illustrates all kinds of ethics and duties for everyone—from mighty kings to ordinary folks—and their rights as well and also the rasping operation of aforesaid binary oppositions in the society. We realize that whatever the moral values and ethical obligations exhorted in *Tirukkuṟaḷ*, "the Universal Scripture," have been seemingly reminisced either sparingly or elaborately in other Tamiḻ ethical works such as *Nālaḍiyār, Paḻamoḻi Nāṉūṟu, Nāṉmaṇik-kaḍigai, Ciṟupañcamūlam, Tirikaḍugam, Ēlādi*, etc. In such deliberations, we notice a huge influence or heavy dose of tenets and moral codes put forth by Jainism and Buddhism. Contrary to these heterogeneous thoughts, the *Ācārakkōvai* (*ĀK*) so diligently had exhorted almost all moral values, ethical codes and practices endorsed by the Vedic Hinduism in its 100 verses.

The ethical codes and practices of Hinduism that are supposed to be strictly followed in the day-to-day life—from awakening phase to sleeping stage—by the first three *varṇas*[6] (*brāhmiṇs, kshatriyas* and *vaishyas*) are very systematically divulged in this peculiar work. And the ethical composition has cited certain austere observances to be firmly adhered to and some irreverent adherences not to be ever observed by the men of three *varṇas* in their 'inner' (home) and 'outer' (public) spheres which would guarantee the so-called 'salvation' after the worldly life. While the austere and contemptuous observances related to waking, bathing, worshipping, eating, sleeping and so on that one needs to adhere to in his/her 'inner sphere' are insisted upon in the early part of the work, other adherences such as walking, studying, listening, speaking, behaving, and so on that one needs to conduct himself/herself in the 'outer spheres,' viz. royal palace/royal court, assembly of learned, council of elders, school/institution, and so on, are pressed in the later part of the book. The prominent people—who have strong stake in land, religion, politics, education, etc.—especially kings and priests/*brāhmiṇs* are the central figures mostly referred to in this ethical volume. Others such as women and labourers who sweat hard and toil more in homes, lands, mountains and forests do not find place in the didactic composition. "Concept of Purity," the age-old fortress of the Brāhmaṇism, built upon the basement, viz. holy *vs.* profanity, clean *vs.* pollution has been interspersed profoundly in every verse of the ethical work. It is not wise to say that there exist scientific values or real-world veracities to the orthodox codes and practices uttered in the ethical works in general, *Ācārak-kōvai* in particular. We could realize that the so-called remarkable precept of Hinduism, viz. *svarg–narak* (heaven–hell) philosophy—built upon the foundation of *goodness vs. wickedness*—is dynamically functioning as the basis for whole lot of orthodox codes and practices.

Between King and Citizens:
Relationships/Interactions

When the conception of "Right to hold Property" emerged in the bygone era, inevitably there arose countless violent events between the divergent Tamil clans who dwelt on mountains, forests, cultivable plain lands, seacoasts and wastelands. The mightiest man among them was duly acknowledged as the lord/king of their clan. Eventually, the king got bestowed 'the Ultimate Power' sooner in order to streamline/control the barbarous activities of his subjects. The final period of the rough and tough attitudes of clan culture is termed 'Heroic Age' (*c.* 3000 BCE–300 CE) in the scheme of periodization. "It is said that the ruling institution called 'the government,' indeed, came into existence in this period" (Raj Gauthaman, *Ibid.*, p. 197).

The lord of the clan who got conferred colossal powers was later known as *arasan* (king), *kō* (king), *mannan* (king), *vēndan* (king/monarch), and *irai* (lord). Only he was entitled to act as the lord of his people. The lord was expected to be prodigious in education, knowledge and action besides an exceptional man conducting himself excellently in the spheres of mind, speech and deed. His action of mighty physique was hailed as *ānmai* (prowess)/*vīram* (valour)/*maram* (bravery). His deeds of compassion were greeted as *mānbu* (honour)/*īgai* (benevolence)/*aram* (virtue). These two royal qualities (prowess and benevolence) were considered as the two eyes of a king. "All works are agreed that the first and foremost duty of the king is the protection of his subjects. *Śāntiparva* (68. 1–4) notes that all the seven expounders of polity (*rajaśāstrapranetārah*) named by it extol protection as the highest *dharma* of the king. Manu (VII. 144) states that the protection of subjects is the highest *dharma* and Kālidāsa in *Raghuvaṁśa* 14.67 alludes this dictum of Manu. Protection consists in punishing internal aggression (such as by thieves and robbers and by persons who invade a man's rights) and in meeting external aggression" (Kane 1946: 56). And "Gauthama (X. 7–8) prescribes that the special responsibility of the king is to protect all beings, to award just punishment and that he has to protect the several *varṇa*s and *āśrama*s according to the rules of *śāstra* and to bring them round to the path of their proper duties when they swerve from it (XI. 9–10)" (Kane, *Ibid.*). Nevertheless, this sort of notion on king is not seen with such attributes even scarcely in *Ācārakkōvai* but denoted with some other qualities. The king is just referred to in this work as *arasaṉ* (*ĀK* 16), *iṟaivaṉ* (*ĀK* 78).

In this ethical work, several attributes related to God and temple have been clearly equated with the king and the palace. The royal court or the royal palace is reverently referred to as *kōvil* > *kōyil* (< *kō* = king + *il* = residence, i.e., 'the royal palace') which predominantly meant 'temple' till the advent of British. Since the royal home of king too has the same supreme power of protecting or destroying people and the sanctity bestowed upon it, the dwelling place of monarch is equated with the temple. Similarly, just as devotees reverently worship their Gods while placing the Almighty in the supreme plane at temple, the people of country too just keep their king at the highest pedestal bestowing him with the sovereign powers and respect him with fear and awe, so states the *Ācārakkōvai*. The supreme reigning power is just akin to the fire—when someone goes so near/interacts so closely with this 'live wire' then he/she instantly or sooner will be burnt/ruined due to his/her fault. When interacting with the king—'the Supreme Authority'—people must remain extremely mindful and vigilant. Because, whatever entities function in such domain of the ultimate authority, naturally do possess the devastating characteristics of the fire. So, "No one should get angry even when an ordinary soldier stops him/her at the gate of royal court from entering" (*ĀK* 66), thus cautions the didactic text. This is because the anger of a devotee or an individual has no effect on God or the lord, not even on the person who enjoys the blessings of the ultimate power. On the contrary, such fury would only bring misery upon the individual. Anyone who goes to the temple seeking 'the grace of the Almighty,' generally, is expected not to go with high decoration than the God. Similarly, "someone paying a visit to the king should not go wearing more extravagant dresses and extra ornamentation than the monarch" (*Ibid.*). "No one should spend more amount of money for carrying out any activity like charity, conducting wedding, indulging in business, constructing house and so on than the king though a person is so rich possessing enormous wealth. If anyone violates this ethos then his wealth would vanish in no time," thus warns another verse (*ĀK* 85).

It is believed that constructing a house taller than the temple is a sinful act. Also no one should celebrate any of his family functions with more grandeur than the temple festivals. Showing disregard to this ethic is nothing but an evil act. Usually, no devotee goes to temple with empty hands. It is considered a sacrilegious act. So, everyone earnestly carries a bunch of flowers, fruits, coconuts, camphor, etc., as items for ritualistic worship to invoke the God for His grace. Similarly, "while visiting the king too, people *ought to take* whatever gift is possible along with them that merits their social status and economic condition. This is indeed an ethical act endorsed by elders" (*ĀK* 66). In the temple no *bhakta should exercise* excessive liberty while praying to the God. No one *should not stand* in front facing the God. Instead, standing aside gently, the person should reverently place his/her worries while worshipping. It is exactly in this manner, "without taking more liberty" (*ĀK* 66), and "not uttering any words of pride over one's achievement in education, earned wealth, and fine characteristics, and more notably not elucidating anything unnecessarily" (*ĀK* 71), the subject *ought to convey* his/her state of thought quietly, and in few words to the king. "Whatsoever may be his/her grievances worse yet the person *should not express* it to the king when he is standing alone in a place. Though the matter would fetch gains, the person should not voluntarily convey the problem to the king" (*ĀK* 69), thus further adds the ethical text.

The king always expects his subjects to behave with dis cipline, dignity, and responsibility. Hence, the *Ācārakkōvai* insists, "people *must stay away* from doing certain things such as spitting, sitting on larger chair, chewing betel leaves with areca nut, expressing unentitled matters, and sleeping in front of the king" (*ĀK* 70). Further it adds, "the people *ought to avoid* also laughing, yawning, and sneezing. Otherwise, they would stay as blasphemy forever" (*ĀK* 73). Besides these odd behaviours, the following errant actions of people such as "going in the middle of royal court and taking a seat next to someone where the king was also present" (*ĀK* 66), and "engaged in surreptitious talk with someone" (*ĀK* 78) were also considered disgraceful acts. Furthermore, "standing clo-sely with the king in the royal court, and eavesdropping on the king's conversation with someone" were considered very serious outrageous acts. "When such situation arises, the person should behave as if he is looking for something else there" (*ĀK* 78). Everyone ought to concentrate on their own affairs, not on those of others. Else such kinds of actions would be construed having ulterior motives/hidden intentions. As any act of deceit and conspiracy could exterminate the precious life of the king in a fraction of seconds, even a little movement of a person would be very intensely observed by the king as well as his bodyguards. So, everyone needs to amend his body language and words according to the temperament of the king. "Though it is absolutely wrong when the king says that the colour of crow is white, *no one should disagree* with him" (*ĀK* 69), so says another verse from the didactic text. With the references quoted so far, we understand the prescription of the pivotal point which hails the king as "the sole Supreme Power" just on a par with God in all respects.

Etiquette and Ethos of Nobles

The essential attributes of prowess/manhood, especially the *vīram* (valour) and *māṉam* (honour) that prevailed during the 'Heroic Age' witnessed altogether a shift in the "Didactic Literary Works Age" (*c.* 250–600 CE). No word either on heroism or heroic kings were mentioned in the *Ācārakkōvai*. The didactic work just candidly puts forth the phenomenal attributes of kings, *brāhmiṇ*s, landlords and traders as the fine ethical codes and practices adhered by great men. Obviously, the orthodox codes and practices are numerous. However, the *ĀK* (verse 1) considers the following eight moral activities as the seed or root of the traditional ethical codes and practices (*ĀK* 49). They are: 1) Gratefulness, 2) Patience, 3) Uttering nice words, 4) Doing no harm to any being, 5) Education, 6) Benevolence, 7) Wisdom, 8) Friendship with noble men. People's usual dressing sense, walking style or mental atti-tude, and even some negative traits such as disregarding one's own promised words and scolding others too could signify their ethical culture which got materialized on the basis of their qualification, education, prowess/manliness, and family lineage.

Perhaps, in the society of agrarian civilization where individual earned the right of holding property—the nobles, great men and prodigious people, who represented then a small population—might have led the life of self-control and discipline. At times, they could have led a dignified life. However, expecting everyone to behave exactly in the same manner is impractical, rather atypical. In fact, during the post-Sangam period, the term 'education' candidly meant 'the knowledge acquired from Vedas'; the word 'scholar' apparently referred to 'the person who mastered the Vedas.' In ancient time, 'living pious life to the tenets exhorted in four Vedas' was acknowledged as 'ethics' or 'morality.' Conducting the sacrament customs such as *yajña*, *mantra* and *tantra* in the quest of propitiating Gods or for the prosperity of rulers were considered ethics in those days. Only *brāhmin priests* who excelled in education, wisdom and, ethics were recognized as 'great men' or 'prodigious individuals.' As these *brāhmin priests* are considered possessing the 'pure ethics,' the *Ācārakkōvai* insists that "the world *should greet* them wholeheartedly by keeping them on par with their parents on their head" (*ĀK* 61). The ethical text further insists: "When *brāhmin*s are on the pathway, *others ought to give way* by getting aside. Only such fine people are blessed and would be revered by one and all in their every birth" (*ĀK* 64). Since the *brāhmin*s were believed to be "the pious people," even their ordinary utterings were revered as amazing powerful maxims. Therefore, "astute men never consult any *pulaiya* (untouchable) while planning to do a noble deed. But they always consult the impeccable *brāhmin*s and act accordingly to their suggestions as their dictums would never fail" (*ĀK* 92), thus resolutely pronounces the versifier

Peruvāyiṉ Muḷḷiyār. We could realize here the forceful functioning of the notion—which is ordinarily found in the scheme of hierarchal system—"higher *vs.* lower" is deliberated very perceptively on its own terms. How far is this view flawless? Sadly, we are, indeed, clueless!

The physical world wherein we live is the ultimate product of *pañca bhūta*s (five elements of Nature) such as earth, water, fire, wind and ether (space). Numerous beings of different categories are born, evolve, live and perish in mountains, forests, plain cultivable lands, and seacoast regions since evolution. Out of all creatures, it is only the human beings who worship these *pañca bhūta*s either out of fear or devotion. Along with these, "the men of wisdom should adore *brāhmiṇ*s, cow, moon and sun like his own body" (*ĀK* 15), thus endorses the treatise. "Or else, the Gods of *pañca bhūta*s dwelling in his body would leave him to suffer forever" (*Ibid.*), so warns the scripture. Nevertheless, we are unable to understand how the *brāhmiṇ*s and cows also could hold such amazing colossal powers on a par with the *pañca bhūta*s, the moon and the sun. Also how did they get grouped along with the elements of Nature on a high pedestal? A verse in the ethical volume expresses that the *brāhmiṇ*s— "the men of wisdom do possess divinity. Hence, when people happen to see them, they *should stand up* promptly and *should fall at* their feet sincerely. When these men of divinity greet them by saying "Good," then only the people fallen at their feet should stand up. The abovementioned three attributes are, in fact, the essence of ethical codes" (*ĀK* 62). Another verse states, "The *tiṟaṅkaṇḍār* (the erudite people) always adore ascetics" (*ĀK* 63). "The *aruṅkēḷviyavar*, 'the men of wisdom' (mostly *brāhmiṇ*s, and other learned and prodigious people) while present in the middle of a council neither disparage nor insult anyone; *do not sleep* in the middle of many people;

would not hide themselves in a corner after having accepted a task to discharge yet unsuccessful in their attempt; they *don't scorn* anyone those who are absent in the gathering" (*ĀK* 50), thus another verse canvasses the image of great men in high esteem. The implication behind this sketching is two-fold. The didactic work on the one hand asserts that the *brāhmiṇs* happened to be the nobles customarily, while the lower strata people, mostly the untouchables, happened to be ignobles on the other hand. The Vedic Hinduism keeping its very 'notion of purity' on a high pedestal, in a way, discreetly mocks the underprivileged as people of not having any qualm to sleep in the middle of the crowd, dishonest to their own statements, and very much ill-mannered. Contrary to this reading, the orthodox creed acclaims that "the *aiyamil kāṭciyavar* ('the visionaries of doubtless mind,' 'the men of acumen,' i.e., 'the *brāhmiṇs* and other great men') in front of the elders wouldn't speak imprudently by pointing their finger/hand at something against them; wouldn't scribe anything by their foot; wouldn't compare critically a person not present with someone sitting in the gathering; would not take anything in the sitting posture when noble/elderly people offer something to them" (*ĀK* 94). "These *tiṟankaṇḍār* (the erudite people) feel bashful for such disgraceful acts" (*ĀK* 63); "they *wouldn't make* any excessive gesticulation; *wouldn't walk* dropping any dirt; *wouldn't speak* harsh words in the council of the learned; even *wouldn't go* to the place where two persons are engaged in conversation" (*ĀK* 93). Yet in another verse the ethical text states, the *asaiyāda uḷḷattavar*, (the men of unwavering mind), the burgess men from higher class would not utter—any deceitful word, useless term, any word in impertinent way or disrespectful manner, and disparage words—and also, they wouldn't indulge in backbiting" (*ĀK* 52).

The *Ācārakkōvai* further adds, the *neṟippaṭṭavar* (the people adhering to tradition), i.e., 'the people of higher principles,' not only in the councils/assemblies even in other places too *would act* or *behave* with sheer poise and total dedication" (*Ibid.*). "These people *don't throw* any item, or a stone; neighing and calling someone out loudly who is away at distance. They *don't deride* anyone; *don't get angry* over others; *don't hide* themselves; *don't clap* their hands; *don't wink* their eyes at someone or move their nose to sides" (*ĀK* 53). "As these *kaḍaṉaṟi kāṭciyavar* (the visionaries well versed in customs), the people of excellent traits highly honour the notion of 'purity'/'veneration,' they *don't walk* in between two lights and two people; *don't spit* on walls. Even at their worst suffering times, they *don't wear* other's dirty clothes either to cover the lower part or the upper part of their body respectively. And they *don't take off* their dress when happening to be in the middle of a public place. Even they are very cautious enough that the smell of their dress does not reach or cause others to feel sick" (*ĀK* 36), so *Ācārakkōvai* renders more details about the fine qualities of pious people in a verse. In a similar vein yet in different tone, another verse also asserts these facts as follows. "One *should not untie* his dress in public; *should not scratch* his ear; *should not speak* raising his hand; *should not look* at women; *should not eavesdrop* while a person is sharing a secret with another" (*ĀK* 75). Here, we could notice that more or less the same facts are divulged in the above mentioned two verses 36 and 75, however, in two kinds of tenor. According to the versifier Peruvāyiṉ Muḷḷiyār, all these traits are not the conducts of cultured ones.

Generally, great men—especially the *brāhmiṇs* who emerge from the backdrop of disciplines such as education, ethics, and wisdom and serve within those domains—naturally possess a sense of fear or apprehension. Understandably, this apprehension includes concern for their own lives, possessions (such as cattle, land, buildings, money, jewelry, etc.), and personal honour or dignity. Hence, these *nigaril arivinār* (the unparalleled knowledgeable people), 'the excellent learned men' *don't stay* for a long time at the dangerous battle ground, toddy/arrack shops where drunkards lay down after losing their consciousness, slum of whores, the place where once friends turned thence foes assembled, and flight of steps leading to water from the bank of a river, pond, etc." (*ĀK* 55). We can reasonably grasp the potential dangers lurking in the places mentioned above. In locations such as battlefields and toddy shops, riots or violent disturbances may erupt at any moment for various reasons. Since these learned men are evidently not equipped to confront such threats with physical strength, they are likely to leave these areas as quickly as possible. Although they are recognised for their mental resilience, prolonged exposure to deplorable environments—such as toddy shops and brothels—could undermine their psychosomatic stability. Even if they remain composed in such places, their integrity may come under suspicion, leading them to be labeled as 'men of immorality' or 'impropriety.' Therefore, in every sense, it is wise for well-educated individuals to avoid such places altogether or leave well before any risk escalates. It is because of this knowledge, "these wise men *don't stay* in the region where well dried-up grasses are overgrown; *don't put* them into fire" (*ĀK* 56). The reason behind this, perhaps, could be the vulnerabilities arising from poisonous reptiles like scorpions, snakes, etc., and also the potential risk from wildfire. The sensible people "*don't go* into the forest alone" (*Ibid.*). Because possibly they could be attacked and killed at times by wild animals and reptiles.

Apparently, prudent people are aware of all these hazards. So, these astute people, "*don't run fast* with wide steps in rains" (*Ibid.*), as they possibly end up with fractures by falling on the ground. Obviously, these people *don't risk their life* by indulging in any sort of daring activities. These sagacious people utterly believe the notions related to the subjects such as God, celestials, *bhūtas, puṇyas, pāpas,* etc., expressed in the Vedas. So, "they *don't stay* alone in the places like ruined house, temple, graveyard, and under the lone dried-up tree withering in the dilapidated open space" (*ĀK* 57). They strongly believe that evil spirits like *bhūtas* and ghosts inhabit such dilapidated places and may cause them harm. So perceptively, they avoid staying alone in such places. However, it is perplexing to see the temple—the divine abode of God—grouped alongside the abandoned house, dreadful graveyard, and the barren tree, in the list of uninhabited places. It is construed that violating this adherence is nothing but an act of *pāp* (sin). Therefore, "even at the worst situation of poverty, these people *don't deviate* from their community lineage which strikingly adores such ethical codes and practices. Rather, they strictly follow those moral principles at any cost in their day to day lives too" (*ĀK* 56). For instance, "they *don't sleep* even for a little interval during the day times even though they feel utter tiredness, if they wish to stay away from diseases" (*ĀK* 57). It is their customary belief that the inauspicious act would hand down diseases to them and *darittiram* (utter poverty or absolute destitution) as well.

Naturally, other people too would wish to achieve excellence in life like the great elders principled and matured with wisdom who had reached a superior level. For this accomplishment, "the ordinary men while accompanying the elders *should not go sitting* (on the mount of horse, elephant, etc.) in a vehicle; besides they *should not go* wearing footwear and holding umbrella to save them from the scorching sun" (*ĀK* 60). It is believed that the wrath of great elders principled and matured with wisdom is akin to that of Gods. So as to stay away from the elders' wrath, "the other men *should give way* to the people carrying luggage, patients, elders, children, cows, women above and beyond they must give pathway to *brāhmin*s and *tapasi*s (ascetics), if they really wish to accomplish the good fortune" (*ĀK* 64). "A person who wishes to greet such great elders in the quest of seeking their blessings *should not walk* into the middle of processions and venerate/worship at royal palaces and temples respectively where king and gods do rounds" (*ĀK* 72). Violating this ethics is considered sheer foolishness. Because the aforementioned respectful public places had assumed to have contained 'the purity' as well as 'Supreme Power' together. So, the serenity of these reverend sites should not lose their sanctity at the cost of someone's excitement cum troubling activities. In order to safeguard the sanctity of the above-mentioned abodes, the sensible man *should pay his respect* to elders/great men from the very location wherever he is standing away. Nevertheless, this act cannot be construed as disregard. However, "in other locations, be it even a forest, one *should not sit* haughtily, or cross-legged when elders are present there. Besides, the person *must not sleep* covering his body with a blanket without extending the same gesture to elders well beforehand. Negating this culture is indeed presumed as perimeter of contempt" (*ĀK* 91). Further, the *Ācārakkōvai* cautions that *no one should disregard* elderly people perceiving them as aged and can't do any harm to him/her. It reasons out, "if a person dishonours the following four entities—a snake alive in anthill, king, fire, and a lion living in cave—taking them as tender, docile and friendly, then misery will occur" (*ĀK* 84). So, a person needs to be ever conscious and act responsibly in his/her life, if he/she wishes to lead a good life devoid of moral consequences of vicious deeds.

Teachers and Pupils: Interaction/Relationship

Māta-Pita-Guru-Deyvam (Mother-Father-Teacher-God)—thus Sanskrit tradition pronounces the line of veneration in descending order. *Aṇṇaiyum pitāvum muṉṉari deyvam* (Mother and father are the earliest known gods), so says similarly, a poetess Avvaiyār in her ethical work *Koṉrai Vēndaṉ,*[7] yet with little difference. Apparently, every society—of all the kith and kin—gives prime importance or primary respect to 'mothers.' But the ethical text *Ācārakkōvai* strikingly renders the adorable group in a different manner as follows. "One should venerate the incomparable mentors, viz. king, teacher, mother, father, and elder brother like the way one worships the celestials/gods" (*ĀK* 16). In this line of adoration, it is to be noted that prime importance is given to 'the king' followed by 'the teacher' who was placed well before the 'the mother,' universally the most valued and lovable person. Then positioned are one's father and elder brother in the fourth and fifth places respectively. Apparently, the didactic work places 'the king' in the highest pedestal. Perhaps, the unquestionable supreme power of the king and the vital intellect of the teacher, as witnessed during the heroic period, might have compelled the author to place the monarch above even one's own mother and father. It is to be realized that the worship of God is, in fact, implicitly placed (through the terms like the way one worships the celestials/gods) at the very first place well before all others. Strangely somehow 'the elder brother,' a senior sibling of a person, also gets into the list of veneration line. Otherwise, 'the mother' and 'father,' the highly esteemed endearing figures were not given due importance in the ethical composition. Nonetheless, the *īnṟāḷ* (the who one borne the child) has been just mentioned in another context in the verse (*ĀK* 65).

"Man is a social being," as has been often mentioned by sociologists elsewhere. It is quite natural that human beings also do inherit some typical qualities of animals to some extent. Humans allegedly had remained barbaric for several hundred centuries since evolution. Over time, they gradually shed their animalistic traits, particularly their brutish instincts. Subsequently, they became domesticated and civilized in the days then followed. Consequently, they started outlining certain norms, rules and regulations in the quest for interacting and maintaining bonds with kith and kin, viz. mother, father, brother, sister, aunt, uncle and others. During the period of civilization, there also emerged nitty-gritty of sanctions and restrictions related to man's sexual life. While the man has been allowed to have the physical relationship with grown up females in general, yet he has been regulated not to have the same liaison with women closely connected to him by blood by citing some ethical codes and practices as taboos. Though such taboos are not identical in all ethnicities, no culture allows a man to have sexual relationship either with his mother, or sister, or daughter. Incongruously, bringing colossal damage to the prevailing culture, certain unethical activities allied to physical intercourse have arisen among human beings out of animal instincts at times. To stay away from such bizarre and illegitimate actions, the *Ācārakkōvai* forbids "a man from residing with any woman who is alone at a house/home, be she is his own mother, or sister or daughter" (*ĀK* 65). This could be because of the ID (Impulses and Desire) factor, which is often uncontrollable in certain situations for individuals who are mentally or emotionally weak. Those situations would obviously make them become victims of circumstances either apprehensively or wilfully. Except in this verse, mother or father or any kith was not referred in any other verse. Why is it so? It is interesting for our speculation. More than the references (something or other directly) made on kings and *brāhmiṇ*s, the overwhelmingly mentioned people are "the excelled men who adhered to orthodox codes and principles." The people of this category are admired as *āynda aṟiviṇar* (the intellectuals who explored subjects), 'the erudite men of wisdom,' *āṉṟavinda mūtta viḻumiyār*, 'the wise and self-possessed elderly excellent men,' *cevviyār*, 'the nobles,' etc. These individuals were most likely the *brāhmiṇ*s well-versed in the Vedas and staunch followers of orthodox principles.

The only other category of men finding place in this pious lot is *upāddiyāyaṉ* (< Skt. *upādhyāy* meaning 'a teacher' in general, 'a spiritual preceptor' in particular). The teachers, who are also known by other names such as *ācārya, guru, upādhyāy*, happened to be mostly the *brāhmiṇ*s in the socio-history of India. Since the 'Vedic Age' (*c.* 1500–500 BCE) till the days of colonial period, 'education' in India conspicuously meant 'the knowledge of Vedas.' Those who taught the Vedas then were duly recognized as 'Gods.' In the abovementioned period, except *shūdra*s, the people from three *varṇa*s (*brāhmiṇ*s, *kshatriya*s, and *vaishya*s) did acquire the Vedic education by leaving their homes and living with their respective *guru*s (teachers) for a few years. The main focus was on Vedic education, yet the *sishya*s (pupils) were taught several subjects and divergent disciplines. They were also trained in fine arts and martial arts. It is said that the students then gradually progress into complete manhood when they come out of their *gurukul*s.[8] So, apparently, the pupils did respect their *guru*s reverentially by keeping them on a par with the Almighty. The students also showed the utmost modesty towards their masters; rendered whatsoever sacrifices required for their masters' comfort. It goes without saying that the relationship that prevailed between the *guru* and his pupils during those times was similar to that of between the God and the devotees, king and his subjects. There are a quite number of instances in *Ācārakkōvai* which clearly corroborate the above statement. "A virtuous student *should stand* in front of the teacher with modesty. He *should not leave* the place before hearing the word 'go' from the teacher. When the teacher engages in the class, the student *should be* more attentive by lending his ears completely. While the teacher does not reply to his query whatsoever, the pupil then *should not ask* him again," thus *ĀK* outlines the virtues to be adhered by students in classrooms. As students are young lads, unable to read the actual situation of circumstances, they may convey something to the teacher out of context at times. Besides, there is every chance that students might be nervous and fumble to express something coherently out of fear. Nonetheless, it is quite natural. To save oneself from such unpleasant situations, *ĀK* prescribes, "A student while expressing something to the teacher concerned *should not be* in a hurry; *should not repeat* over and again the same thing; *should not* utter lies by stretching but *should convey* whatever matter precisely in appropriate situation" (*ĀK* 76).

In the bygone era, *guru*s did not accept/get any fee from their *shisya*s for imparting education. However, the pupils before leaving their *āshram*s used to offer the *gurudakshiṇa*, (the token fee paid to a spiritual preceptor), a traditional gesture of acknowledgement, respect and thanks to the *guru*, whatsoever possible to their ability. In those days, the academic activity called 'Learning' was like conducting *yajña* (worship performed with sacrificial fire) where the priest(s) had been suitably awarded *saṉmāṉam* (< *saṉmāṉ* or *sammāṉ*, [Skt.]), 'the reward' at the end of the successful event.

Similarly, pupils had offered something special to their *gurus* before leaving their *gurukul*s, the residential schools. This gifting is known as *gurudakshina* in Vedic culture. It is an irony that the acclaimed *guru* Droṇāchārya had demanded the thumb of the right-hand and got it severed from Eklavya, a young prince of Nishadha—a confederation of jungle tribes in Ancient India—for the archery tutelage that the erstwhile *guru* who had indeed not taught the archery to him. *Ācārakkōvai*, the earliest Tamiḻ ethical book of *Hindu Dharma*, persistently says, "A pupil *should offer gurudakshina* with utmost earnest and sheer reverence to *guru*, wholly with no contraction between his mind, words and deeds, in the manner a virtuous person conducts himself engaged with learning, indulging in *tapas* (penance), and conducting the *yajña*" (*ĀK* 3). The ethical text insists that a pupil *should conduct* himself in the above said manner for his own interest as the academic and non-academic disciplines were taught free by the erudite *guru*. Else, the work warns that the student would suffer with *kēḍu* (misery) forever. "If anyone wishes to lead the life constantly with no distress then the person *should protect* his own body, wife, subject sheltered, and wealth/property the way he safeguards the gold. Otherwise, sheer misery would engulf him" (*ĀK* 95), thus it cautions. 'Warning'/'Cautioning' with dire consequences is a trademark feature of all ethical works. Though the *Ācārakkōvai* follows this strictly, it employs a juxtaposed strategy, i.e., *if you observe this, do this, you will reap this benefit* to encourage people for following certain Vedic codes and practices in their day-to-day lives as entrepreneurs do invite investment from public and quoting the prospective profit in return on such endeavour in their business. It assures the people that they would obtain all the fruits of the tree called *aishvaryam* (opulence) if they adhere honestly to the Vedic *dharma*s cited. "The one who observes all the *dharma*s mentioned in *Dharmaśāstra*s with firm and total commitment would gain wealth and will be handsome or fine-looking in this birth. Also, he would become a landlord and a learned man. His words would be respected by one and all. Besides, the person would live long without any disease in this world" (*ĀK* 2). The didactic treatise guarantees the people whoever observe sincerely the 'dharmic life' that they would be blessed ones, not only in their present birth but also would remain, so that they would be born in *naṟkuḍi* ('noble family'/'clan') in the forthcoming births.

Orthodox Codes and Practices

Not everyone is fortunate to lead the same kind of life, and the reasons for this are manifold. The socio-political and religious environment into which a person is born, as well as the specific place and time of their upbringing, largely shape their present life. It is on these foundational factors that an individual's civilization, culture, and thought are fundamentally built.

In the post-Sangam age, the heterogeneous religions, viz. Buddhism and Jainism on the one hand and the Hinduism on the other, have interpreted human's life differently as per their own doctrines. So, they prescribed dissimilar codes and practices to mankind. "The world, the life, youthfulness, wealth, body etc., are naturally impermanent. They are bound to fall off/to become extinct from the world. So, man should not develop desire/attachment over them. Rather, he should evolve as a fine human being with austerity. At the end, his journey into the world should be free by renunciation and abandonment of all worldly pleasures. That is the blissful state called "Nirvāṇa" to be attained by "Kevala Jnāna" ('Realization'/'Enlightenment').[9] For accomplishing this highest state, every human being should strive hard by austere means," thus outlines Jainism. In its scheme, **there exists no**

'Godhead' or 'the Creator of the Universe.' But "it believed in the existence of 'Perfect Souls' abiding in the highest region of the world with fully developed consciousness. It gave much importance to *karma* theory. To escape from the bondage of birth and death, it advocated that the *jiva* should control his sense of material life and develop spiritualized austere life" (Rajagopal 2007: 151). In a similar vein yet with difference, Buddha ('The Enlightened One,' 563–480 BCE), who out rightly rejected the notion of God like his predecessor Mahavīra ('The Great Warrior,' 599–527 BCE), preached his gospel and termed it "Nirvāṇa" ('Liberation'). As the Bodhi, he put it, **"the desire for personal gratification was the root cause of all sorrows in the world and that the only way to end sorrow was to extinguish all selfish desires"** (*Ibid.*, p. 150). Whereas the Vedic Hinduism strongly believed and propagated that **"human welfare and even the existence of the world depended upon the utter mercy of the deities whose favour could be sought through sacrificial rites and rituals"** (*Ibid.*, p. 151). The much-admired *rishi*s of Vedic period like Manu and Bhrigu had expounded that the man can accomplish the delightful state called *mukti* forever by sincerely observing all *dharma*s cited in the Vedic *Śāstra*s. All the three creeds unanimously professed that it is because of the (mis)deeds of a person's previous birth that he or she is actually coming back to the world once or several times again. Bringing down the curtain to the recurring play of *karma,* i.e., the *mukti* (the cessation of birth cycle) is possible, if the person is conscious enough and strictly follows the ethical codes and practices expounded in Vedas and *Śāstra*s. The deeds are classified as *ācāra*s (good behaviours/customs) and *anācāra*s (evil deeds or misdeeds/bad behaviours) by their nature. However, certain *ācāra*s had to be observed only by certain castes as expressed as *varṇāśrama dharma* in *Dharmaśāstra*s. When there is defilement, then the same *ācāra*s turn out to be *anācāra*s. For instance, *shūdra*s and *atishūdra*s (*Dalit*s) were not entitled either to study or listen to Vedas till the advent of the British. If they violate this ethic, then their act becomes not only misdeed but a sin. So, these marginalized men were cruelly punished, their ears were filled with lead and tongues were severed, whenever they transgressed the tenents.

It is firmly believed that when the soul leaves the body, the good and bad conducts of that being also sail along with the soul to 'the abode of God' or 'Celestials.' Upon reaching there, their good and bad deeds are weighed. The cessation of birth cycle or the next probable birth of the beings ranging from one sense to six senses is determined according to the measure of good and bad deeds performed by that being. Thus, till the clearance of all misfortunes earned during birth(s), all the beings do experience pleasures and pains, of course, in varying degrees. When all the *karma*s get removed, the soul becomes 'liberated.' The soul, according to Vedic Hinduism, ascending from the lower to the higher *varṇa*, finally merges again with 'the Absolute Being' and becomes 'a pure soul' living in an everlasting blissful condition at the abode of celestials known as *moksha*. They duly reach the state of *Arihant* (The One who has destroyed his inner enemies such as greed, anger, desire, and hatred) or "Buddhahood" ('The Enlightenment') respectively in the case of Jainism and Buddhism. Apparently, **the goal of all beings is to get rid of the birth and death cycle** just in the quest of escaping to the unknown sphere beyond from the dependence of time and place. For this accomplishment, the respective religions and their God's grace are essential. The decree for acquiring this grace is, "all beings should behave like the ideal citizens of the god" (Raj Gauthaman, *Op. cit.*, pp. 91–92).

Morning Activities: *Ācāram*s (Virtuous Acts)

According to the Vedic *ācāram*, "One *should wake up* from sleep in the early morning so as to get the grace of God" (*ĀK* 4). Then, "*One should worship* standing in the cold water with the thinking over the God" (*ĀK* 9). "Soon after awakening in the early morning, one *ought to first pay his respect* to his parents by prostrating before them. Only then the person *should think* of earning wealth in a righteous manner and carry out other virtuous activities of the day" (*ĀK* 4). "*One has to worship* God in the evening too by sitting position on the ground (worshipping god in standing position is sacrilegious)," (*ĀK* 9). Perceivably, we notice here the God and God related matters are occupying a significant portion in whatsoever ceremonial observances stated above. Conspicuously, *these utterings seemed to be authored by a brāhmin for brāhmins.*

Usually, manual labourers do not bathe in the mornings; nor do they typically engage in religious worship at that time. After toiling throughout the day and becoming physically exhausted, they take hot water baths in the evening. The bathing culture is in no way ritualistic one related to God or religious observances as found in the case of *brāhmin*s. The manual workers, unless and otherwise required, generally don't bathe during daytime but mostly after sunset particularly before dinner. If they become dirtied by sweat, dust, or mud then they go for daytime bathe in wells, ponds, lakes and rivers. While bathing in the abovementioned water sources, they often engage in swimming. Their swimming activities are accompanied by shouting and cheering and spitting and splashing, jumping and diving, submerging and resurfacing, spinning side to side, and wading among others playful, though somewhat organized manner. Typically, men—including labourers—wear a piece of cloth while bathing, though at times, they may bathe without even a loin cloth. In such practices, there is no place for notions of virtue or sin. Whereas the Vedic culture not only treats such actions as *aṉācār* (evil deeds or misdeeds/bad behaviours) but also imposes its deific ideology of "pure *vs.* impure" over water. In its purview, "*āynda aṟiviṉar* (the intellectuals who explored subjects), the erudite men of wisdom while bathing in the pond and similar water bodies they *don't swim* hastily; *don't spit* in the water; *don't go down* under water; *don't play*; *don't bathe* just up to the neck though their hairs dry without oil" (*ĀK* 14); "*don't see* reflection of their own bodies" (*ĀK* 13). The people who violate these *ācāram*s, according to the Vedic dictum, are not men of wisdom, which implicitly refers to the 'people of lower class'/'low castes.' As per its sanctions or injunctions, people cannot bathe as and when they desire to. But *Ācārakkōvai* insists, "People, whether they wish or otherwise, *must bathe* before worshipping God, after evil dream, when became polluted, after vomiting, after haircut or head tonsure, before eating, after waking, after sexual union, after the bodily contact with untouchables, after urinating and defecating" (*ĀK* 10). Evidently, observing all these *musts* wholly are impractical even to an ardent adherent of orthodox Hinduism. **It is really sad that the so-called men of wisdom seemed to have no time for attending to any other work/duty except bathing for a number of times in a day.** On top of it all, the irony is that the people of Vedic Hinduism, the non-inhabitants who came all the way from some unfamiliar regions (Central Asia [Iran], Southern Russia near Caspian Sea, South-East Europe in Austria and Hungary) after 500 BCE to Tamiḻ country (South India), unscrupulously did castigate the aborigines (Dravidians/Tamiḻs) of Tamiḻ land as 'outcasts.'

*Eccil*s (Pollutions) and *Ācāram*s (Virtuous Acts)

The *Ācārakkōvai* candidly expounds certain deeds of people as *eccil*s (otherwise known as *tīṭṭu*s, the pollutions) and *ācāram*s (virtuous acts/good behaviours) and on the basis of *Dharmaśāstra*s' doctrines. It is a pity that even coming into contact physically with 'lower class people' is branded as one of the *eccil*s in *ĀK* (verse 10). Even kissing, an ordinary sensual act is also bracketed under this category as an act of *eccil*, 'the pollution' by the ethical text (*ĀK* 7). "The *eccilār*, 'the pure persons' *wouldn't even look at pulaiyaṉ* ('an outcaste person' due to their food culture of eating mutton, beef, fork, fish, etc.), moon, sun, dog, and the star falling" (*ĀK* 6). Looking at these entities is amply *aṉācāram* (misdeeds), 'an act of contamination' according to the didactic work. How *pulaiyaṉ*, the man who toils hard in the land like buffaloes/bullocks and like the dogs known for their sense of gratitude came under this category of contaminated entities? We are clueless. Also, we are oblivion as to how the prevailing celestial entities, viz. the moon, sun and star too became the objects of contagion. Besides the aforesaid *eccil*s, the *naṉgu aṟivār* (the upright savants) *don't touch* cow, *brāhmiṇ*, fire, *deva* (God/Celestial body), and crown of head. Touching them is a sinful act. Definitely one *must not do* so" (*ĀK* 6). Hence, "*Mēdaigaḷ*, 'the genius men' or 'prodigies'—after their urination, excretion, physical intercourse, and lip-locking without taking bath—*don't utter anything* (probably scriptures like Vedas, *Dharmaśāstra*s etc.); *don't talk/discourse/sermon/deliver* (possibly any hymns, *mantra*s, ethical principles, religious notions, etc.) and *don't sleep*" (*ĀK* 8).

Similarly, there are numerous such entities/aspects put into the basket termed *eccil*s. "One *must not apply* oil to his body without touching the water even when he is suffering from some disease. After smearing the oil, the person *must not look at pulaiyas* without sprinkling water on his body" (*ĀK* 13). "A person *must not wipe* the oil applied excessively to his head for smearing it on other body parts. One *should not touch* others' soiled cloths; *shouldn't wear* others' slippers even to get rid of sadness or discontentment" (*ĀK* 12); "*shouldn't scratch* ground; *shouldn't stay* under a tree at night" (*ĀK* 13); "*shouldn't brush* teeth with twigs (mostly of banyan or neem tree) and *shouldn't cut* trees during full-moon day" (*ĀK* 17). Likewise, so many *must-nots* and *should-nots* are packed tightly into the small but significant didactic text endorsing the Vedic dogmas. We understand that in some cases—such as not to touch others' soiled cloths, not to wear others' slippers, not to stay under a tree at night, etc.—of course, the notions of hygiene and concern for safety play their role pragmatically to the desired effect but in other cases—such as not to apply oil without touching water, not to look at *pulaiyas* without sprinkling the water, not to scratch ground, etc.—such rationality seemed to be absent. *Perhaps, the so-called 'learned men of Vedic literature' may be knowing the truth scripted between the lines!*

Consumption of Food: *Ācāram*s (Virtuous Acts)

The *Ācārakkōvai* explicitly illustrates certain deeds related to people's food culture some as righteous virtues and some other as bad ones as well. All living beings begin consuming sustenance even during their early developmental stages, whether in shells or wombs. To survive, every creature must consume some form of food—this is a fundamental aspect of their nature. No being can live without food. The living beings habitually take whatever food items are available in their topographical background. The types of food as well as eating habits vary species to species, and person to person. Survival often necessitates one being preying upon another. Not all insects, reptiles, birds, beasts, human beings are equally blessed with abundant foods. While a small section of population enjoys abundant food and wealth, a majority faces scarcity, often going without meals for days. The proletariats, 'the people of working class,' perhaps all over the world, have not been privileged to eat food sitting leisurely either on chairs or on the ground. Labourers typically eat hastily—often just gruel, bread slices, or minimal food—while continuing their works. They don't pay much attention to the sense of hygiene while eating food. In the context of India, especially Tamil Nadu, till recently men worked in plain lands, mountains, forests, and seas and drank the running water typically by gathering it with their palms folded. But according to the custom of *viṉaiyaṟivāḷar,* ('the intelligent men' who are aware of the role of *karma*), this drinking mannerism is contemptible and condemned.

"One *should take* food only after bath or at least after washing foot and hands but before the drying of water" (*ĀK* 19). "Thence, the person *should wipe/fresh* his mouth; sit on the wooden plank; sprinkle the water around the edges of the eating plate. If a person does not adhere to this custom, it is presumed that "he has not really eaten the food but only wiped his mouth; demons would take away those men's food" (*ĀK* 18). "*No one should eat* food in the positions—either by lying down, or by standing or by sitting on cot or in open space. No food item shall be taken excessively" (*ĀK* 23). "While eating one *should sit* facing the east; also, without swaying and moving, not looking at anything, one *should take* the food without talking but praying to the deity"

(*ĀK* 20). Noticeably, the east direction gets importance even in people's daily routine activity as seen above. Perhaps the significance attached to the east may be due to the notion of divinity as schemed in the theology of Hinduism wherein temples and gods are respectively built and fashioned facing the east. Hence, it also rules that people *should take* food only after offering the same duly to God(s). In the divinity of Hinduism, the priests or *brāhmiṇ*s well-versed in Vedic *Śāstra*s and conduct themselves earnestly as per the tenets of *Dharmaśāstra*s have been highly respected next to the God(s). Perhaps recognizing them as *periyār,* 'the great'/'noble men,' the *Ācārakkōvai* restricts, "*No one should sit* alongside the 'honourable men' in a row in feast; *shouldn't eat* before they start eating. Also, *no one should* get up and leave from the row before these noble men finish eating" (*ĀK* 24).

Furthermore, the earliest ethical text on Hinduism prescribes certain rules related to eating food items of different tastes. "One *should start eating* first the sweet (food) items and complete with bitter/astringent taste (food) items. It is only between these two categories of taste items, other flavoured food items should be taken. This is indeed the righteous *ācāram* (virtuous act)," (*ĀK* 25), thus *Ācārakkōvai* dictates the ruling. In the case of drinking water, the rule book asserts, "One *shouldn't drink* the water—by gathering it with the two palms)" (*ĀK* 28). "Even one *shouldn't wash/clean* his mouth either by standing or by still walking in the water" (*ĀK* 35). That is *aṇācāram* (misdeed) in the canon book of *ĀK*. In addition to these rulings, the ethical work also dictates, "After gargling/rinsing his mouth, one *should thoroughly clean* the area of mouth and face thrice by uttering the appropriate *mantra*" (*ĀK* 27). Thus, we notice various scheming plots in which the *mantra*s also become mechanical exercise and performance of redundant.

Urination and Excretion: *Ācāram*s (Virtuous Acts)

In general, every human being aspires to lead a hygienic life within the constraints of their environment. However, perceptions of hygiene—and the practices associated with it—vary significantly over time, across environments, among individuals, cultures, creeds, and nations. While European countries maintain the utmost hygienic environment in their private as well as public spheres, the Asian countries in general are unable to manage the desired clean environment due to several factors. Chief among these is the issue of over population across the Asian continent. Scantly caring for maintaining hygienic environment is the major factor which causes untold health hazards to Indian populace inside the country and damages severcly the reputation of the country outside globally. Our large size population, coupled with inadequate education, unfortunately leads people to engage in distressing acts—such as spitting, urinating, and defecating—in public spaces like schools, bus stations, railway stations, and even in the surroundings of temples, often creating conditions that could provoke nausea or disgust. Besides this grim environment, a sizeable population has been in a profession of begging as a thriving means to live on the spots mentioned above. Of the locations cited above, the shrines/temples—the acclaimed core entity of Vedic theology—in a way have been functioning as the citadels of thriving professions, viz. begging and prostitution for a long time. Nevertheless, the Vedic creed—being the religion of perpetuating the notion of purity/piety since 1500 BCE—advises rather admonishes people where they should not indulge in a set of disgraceful activities that damage the holy atmosphere by every means. To our concern in the interest of upholding the hygienic environment, the *Ācārakkōvai* cites, *"No one should spit or urinate or excrete* at the entities, locations and such as grass, fertile land, cow dung, graveyard, (public) pathway, water source, shrine/temple, the spot where one's shadow reflects, cow shed, and ashes" (*ĀK* 32). It is really heartening to see such a caring sense thus has been echoed in the ethical text though under the notion of *ācāram*s that one should adhered to. Yet, it has peppered a volume of irrational *ācāram*s endorsed by *Dharmaśāstra*s in several verses. "A person *should not urinate or excrete* during the day facing the south, at night towards the north" (*ĀK* 33). "If people urinate or excrete in other directions out of compulsion, then they should imagine themselves that the directions have indeed disappeared to nowhere and hence they have relieved the natural call(s) themselves by staying at mid-air. Yet they should avoid doing so for goodness even though the post of Indra is said to be offered" (*ĀK* 34).

Hospitality: *Ācāram*s (Virtuous Acts)

'Hospitality,' a unique trait of human beings, i.e., 'entertaining guests' is a core living quality found in every culture. Natural-ly, every clan or ethnicity has formed its own manners, means or materials to entertain guests. This concept in Tamiḻ is termed *virundu ōmbal* (Hospitality). The English term 'guest' and the Tamiḻ term *virundu* are however not closely connected to each other in terms of their etymological meanings. *Virundu* (> *Virundiṉar*), a term denoting 'guests' now, indeed referred to *novelty/newness* > *new faces,* i.e., *unknown people* in the Heroic age and post-Sangam period. Thus, entertaining the new people/unknown people/strangers had been termed as *virundōmbal* in Tamiḻ. The Tamiḻ term *virundu/virundiṉar* is denoted as *atithi*[10] in Sanskrit. Entertaining *atithi*s is emphasized in Vedic culture too, as 'a must *ācāram*' (virtuous act) that one needs to observe for heaven's sake but not as 'a desired human'/'corporeal gesture.' "The righteous people *don't put a vessel* (containing rice) on fire just for themselves. They *don't take food* for themselves alone just to live but for the cause of serving others" (*ĀK* 39), thus endorses *ĀK*. While deliberating on the matter of visiting of guests, *Manu Dharma* states, "A *brahmin* can go as a guest to the homes of *kshatriya, vaishya,* and *shudra* at any time. But others are not entitled to go as guests to a *brahmin*'s home" (*Manu Dharmaśāstra* III: 110–12), And the *Dharmasūtra* of Gauthama V. 39–42 and Manu III. 110–12 says, "A *kṣatriya* is not really an *atithi* to a *brāhmaṇa* nor are *vaiśyas* nor *śūdras*" (Kane 1941: 751). According to the *Manu Dharmaśāstra*, "One has to honour guests according to one's ability, that guests are to be preferred according to the order of *varṇas* and that among the *brāhmaṇas*, the *śrotriya* and one who has completely mastered (at least one) recension of the Veda is to be preferred" (*Ibid.*). As mentioned in the *Manu Dharmaśāstra* (III: 99 & 107), "The guest is to be shown honour by going out to meet him, by offering him water to wash his feet, by giving him a seat, by lighting a lamp before him, by giving food and lodging, by personal attendance on him, by offering him a bed and by accompanying him some distance when he departs" (*Ibid.*, p. 752). Also, *Anuśāsana* 7.6 says, "The host *should give* his eye, mind and agreeable speech to the guest, he *should personally attend* on him and *should accompany* guest, when he ("the guest") departs" (*Ibid.*, p. 753). All these virtues are just quoted verbatim in one of the verses of *Ācārakkōvai* (verse 54). Just echoing the *Varṇāśrama Dharma* ideology of upholding the hierarchal system, the *Taittirīya Saṁhita* (2.2.4) refers to the fact that "when a guest comes, hospitality in which ghee abounds, is offered to him and it remarks that one who comes in a chariot and one who comes in a cart are the two most honoured among guests" (Kane, *Ibid.*, p. 749). As it was strongly believed that entertaining the guests would certainly fetch all the fortunes to the present birth as well as to the future one, the *ĀK* underlines, "The people who never deviate from virtues take food only after offering the same to guests, elders, cow, bird, and child" (*ĀK* 21). Further it adds, "The noble men *don't sit* on high raised seat when the guests are eating at their home. They *don't indulge* in any act that aggrieve the guests even though the formers had rendered a volume of miseries improperly" (*ĀK* 40). While insisting people to offer food on special occasions, the ethical text underscores, "A person *must entertain* with food everyone including guests on his wedding day, on a holy day when venerating gods, on the day of *darppaṇam* (Vedic ritual in which libations of water are offered to one's ancestors) on the day of festivals and on the day of *yajña* (worship performed with sacrificial fire)" (*ĀK* 48); *may offer something as dāna* (the act of giving alms/charity) too. It was actually believed that these all would bestow all fortunes on the person who treats people earnestly with food while entertaining them sincerely. It needs to be recalled here that offering food and place besides other facilities for all *virundiṉar* ("new or unknown people") was rightly called *virundōmbal* (entertaining guests) in the ancient Tamiḻ culture. But in Vedic culture, *dāna should be strictly offered* to people (presumably to the priests/*brāhmiṇ*s who are well-versed with Vedas and *Śāstra*s) only who are nobler than the donor. It amply denotes that **the Vedic priests/*brāhmiṇ*s alone are entitled to receive *dāna* from the men of other (their lower) categories but not vice versa**. This has been very clearly stated in *ĀK* as follows: "If a *brāhmiṇ* offers a cow as *dāna* then one *should not re-*

ceive it" (*ĀK* 90). Because *brāhmiṇ*s, as per *Dharmaśāstra*s, the men of higher class are alone rightly qualified to receive *dāna* from the men of lower categories. The latter are unqualified to receive something as *dāna* from the higher ups. Entertaining guests and offering *dāna*, as per the codes of Vedic *śāstra*s, are essentially carried out by one vying for *goodness*. The men who receive such bestowals must be in the position of conferring their *good wishes* or *blessings* on those men in turn. So, a kind of divinity is shrewdly attributed to Vedic priests/*brāhmiṇ*s in the *Dharmaśāstra*s. In such systems, we observe that the hierarchal ideology of the orthodox creed has been actively operating for centuries—perhaps even to this day. In these contexts, *the donors were typically individuals from lower social categories, while the recipients belonged to higher ones.* Any disruption or reversal of this order was believed to result in both parties being burdened with 'sin.' However, this rigid hierarchical notion from Vedic times appears to have undergone a subtle shift in the present day. No Vedic priest nowadays wholeheartedly will go to a lower-class man's home for *dāna* unless the donor is economically well-off and socially/politically a significant person.

Evenings and Nights: *Ācāram*s (Virtuous Acts)

"Dawn to Dusk," as the English idiom rightly puts it, every living being begins its day anew in the morning and ends with fatigue at night. Before darkness sets in, almost all the creatures, including the humans return to their respective dwelling places for the required rest. The evening hours, particularly at sunset, are the most soothing part of the day before it winds down. For a man who toils all day in hills, forests, fields, or along the seacoast under the scorching sun, opportunities for rest are rare. If he finds even a brief moment, he will readily lie down without hesitation or concern even on a barren patch of land or a hardened surface. He wouldn't have any qualm over it. But "a traditional person, who grows with Vedas, *mantra*, and *tantra* by adhering sincerely to ritual observances, must discharge his duties of the day with determined mind like that of constructive ant, weaver bird, and crow. So that the person's *ācāram* (virtuous act) would excel by all means" (*ĀK* 96); "his present life would prosper. Hence, the person who duly respects *ācāram* shouldn't sleep in the evening time" (*ĀK* 29). Besides, "he *should not take* food at sunset. He should put on the light before the darkness. He *shouldn't go* out after dinner" (*ĀK* 29). All these are vilifications of divinity. One *should always discharge* his every deed with the devout feeling. "Even when going to bed a person *should pray* to God with folded hands. He shouldn't lie down keeping his head facing the north and angled directions" (*ĀK* 30). "He *shouldn't go* to bed before drying up of his wetted body" (*ĀK* 19); "he *shouldn't lie down* on the cot placed in front of the doors way" (*ĀK* 22). There are some pragmatic views on the concept of hygiene and rational aspects dotted on the lines, yet the irrational aspects peppered more, actually make them insignificant. One can see its extension when the versifier endorses the view of Vedic perspective saying, "A person *shouldn't wade* between two Gods (in idols) and two *brāhmiṇs*" (*ĀK* 31). Else, it is contempt. We could realize here that the *brāhmiṇs* are equated with Gods by placing them on the same pedestal. This can be further inferred when the text states, "When the noble/prodigious man blesses while one had sneezed, the latter *should duly worship* him" (*ĀK* 31). "*No one should either give* an object to nobles or *take* a thing from them by stretching single hand" (*ĀK* 28).

Homes: *Ācārams* (Virtuous Acts)

All the living beings have some kind of pits/nests/caves/houses as their dwelling place or residence built on their own. Perhaps, the insects might be the pioneers in constructing their own webs/hives/nests. Naturally, humans must have followed suit by constructing huts and houses to protect themselves from life-threatening natural hazards, and potential dangers posed by wild animals and reptiles. Throughout history, individuals who owned a house have been accorded respect across cultures. The size, architectural design, and cleanliness of a home or building often play a significant role in how others perceive and revere its owner. Even sacred spaces—such as shrines, temples, mosques, churches—are often worshipped with deep reverence largely due to their impressive appearances, although it is ultimately 'the divine power' of the deity that inspires true devotion and faith.

Certainly, man is the only being blessed with the intellect of keeping his house in order, in terms of hygiene. And he has the acumen to keep the household things at appropriate places. While the house is just a residence for most people, it is much more than the dwelling plot for others. Incidentally, the Vedic faith too does not treat the house as mere residence. It sincerely believes that like the shrines/temples, the house too possesses the divine qualities. In the *garbhgriha* (sanctum sanctorum) of shrines, the deity resides. Whereas in house/home lives the deity like *brāhmin*. In the canons of Vedic creed, not everyone has the right to enter the shrine/temple. Similarly, not everyone has the privilege to go into the *brāhmin*'s home. The orthodox religion insists that the sanctity of home should be kept in the manner the sanctity of shrine is taken care of. In its scheme, the *brāhmin* is the lord of his *griha* (home). But the onus of up keeping the sanctity of home essentially lies with the wife of *brāhmiṇ*. "She *should wake up* from the bed in the early morning; clean the house by sweeping out the dust, trashes, and garbage; wipe the floor clean by the cow dung liquid-paste; then she *should wash* the blackened dirty utensils; fill the containers/tubs/drums and a cruet-like vessels with adequate water. Following it, then the *brāhmiṇ* lady *should bathe* and wear flowers before start cooking by lighting fire in the stove" (*ĀK* 46). She *should discharge* all these obligations with utmost dedication. She *should protect* the kitchen from any sort of *eccil* (pollution) with the sense of cleanliness. Then she *should offer* the food cooked to deity and take the same later" (*ĀK* 39). When she is working in the kitchen, "she *should not put out* the oil lamps by blowing air from her mouth; *should not put out* the oven while the food is still cooking; *should not warm* her body from the fire of oven" (*ĀK* 59). These all are *aṉācāram*s as stated by the *Ācārakkōvai*.

In a similar fashion of treating the *atishūdra*s—the largest populace of the country—as 'pollutants'/'untouchables,' the traditional Vedic Hinduism considers its own women people too as polluters during the days of their monthly cycle. The *Dharmaśāstra*s forbade *brāhmiṇ* women from staying inside their homes for three days during menstruation. Until recently, they were assigned to stay in cow sheds or backyards during this period. This is what the orthodox religion offered to the womenfolk who toil sincerely from dawn to dusk and gift progenies to the family to which they belong. Apparently, **the space of women and their movement were confined largely with *pūja*, and to the kitchen and bedroom alone**. This was their actual 'inner sphere' sanctioned by the traditional religion. Otherwise, they were denied access to hall even when deliberations on family matters took place. "Keeping away broom, dust and trashes, petals of flowers, old earthen pots, and torn cot from the wedding halls are also insisted as the other duties of traditional *brāhmin* women" (*ĀK* 45).

"The *brāhmin* women observing the virtuous deeds determinedly *never look at* the handsome body of other men except that of her husband" (*ĀK* 77), thus their chastity desired by *brāhminism* is eulogized. Since these women happened to be the virtuous wives of well-learned, "they *don't even look* at their own beautiful bodies. They *don't comb* their hair in front of others; not even they snap their fingers" (*Ibid.*). Thus, a volume of duties and taboos largely meant for women have been inscribed in the ancient ethical text. Keeping the sanctity of home is onus more on the part of women, yet the lord of home also has something to contribute to it. "An erudite *brāhmin*, if really wishes fortune to befall his home, then *don't go* to his home taking *ciṛiyar,* ('the mean minded people,' presumably the lower-class people) along with him" (*ĀK* 68). Other than this, nothing is insisted for a *brāhmin* to take care of the sanctity of his home.

Contrary to this, there are quite a number of activities that virtuous men carry out in the public sphere. Of such activities, learning, chanting/reciting, and making others chant Vedas, besides conducting *yajña* are very important acts. As maintained by Brāhmaṇism, since the Vedas are sacred scriptures, they *shouldn't be chanted* on all the days and at any time. "They *should be recited/chanted* only on those days of *ashṭami* (the eighth day of waxing or waning moon), *amāvāsai* (new moon day), *paurṇami* (full moon day), and *chaturdasi* (the fourteenth day of a month). But they shouldn't be chanted or recited on those days—when the kings were in suffering/distress, when earth quack occurs, when lightning strikes, and when some sort of pollution takes place" (*ĀK* 47). "No traditional man put off *yajña* fire by pouring water into it, when the sacrificial fire was conducted in daytimes" (*ĀK* 33).

"Leading the domestic life rightly bears the true virtue's name" (*TKḺ* 49), thus emphasizes Tiruvaḷḷuvar in his maxims. The men and women who join hands for the sake of family life are like the axle or pins of the cart. Their role is very pivotal and crucial for the world's existence and endurance. The male and female sexes need to have physical relationship for their offspring. The sexual intercourse of man and woman is termed as *maithun* or *sambhog* in Sanskrit/Hindi; *puṇarcci* in Tamiḻ. When humans were in their early days of evolution, their 'sexual activity' must have taken place anywhere, any time at their will. When they became civilized every society charted some codes and practices of morality. Jainism hails "the renunciation" more than the household life. But the Vedic religion gives prominence to family life than the abandonment of life. In its theology, man has to pass through four *āshrama*s (stages) in his life. They are: *Brahmacharya* (celibacy, student stage), > *Grihastha* (householder stage), > *Vanaprastha* (retired, hermit stage) > *sannyāsa* (renunciation, wandering ascetic stage). Under the *āshrama*s scheme,[11] human life was thus divided into four phases. The goal of each period was the fulfillment and development of the individual. A man has to begin his career as a student focusing on education and observing the practice of celibacy. He *has to stay* in the *gurukul* (residence school) where the *guru* lives. After completing formal education and acquiring adequate knowledge of scriptures, philosophy, science, etc., he may move to the next stage, i.e., 'the householder life.' By marrying a lady in this stage, the man *has to take care* of his household responsibilities, raise family, educate his children and deliver virtuous social life. The *grihastha* was considered as the most important of all stages in sociological context. Then slowly he *has to withdraw* from the interest and responsibilities of leading the family life. Finally, he *has to renounce all desires* and move away from his house and wander as an ascetic. Like Jainism, the renunciation is emphasized in Vedic religion too but with little difference. "Renunciation" is the goal of human life in both religions. The "Ultimate Realization" is termed as *nirvāṇ* or *kevalyajñān* in the Jainism, whereas it is *mukti* or *moksha* in Vedic faith.

As per the injunctions of Vedic philosophy, a man cannot have sexual intercourse with his wife as and when and wherever he desires to have so. In this very private business of man too, the Vedic Hinduism gives its rulings. It points out several factors such as deity, day, star, sanctity, etc., to be taken care of when someone wishes to have physical relationship with his lady. "The man who up keeps *ācāram* (virtuous act) shouldn't have sex with his wife at midday, midnight, evening, morning, and also on the days of *tiruvātirai* (auspicious day in regard to Śiva), *tiruvōṇam* (auspicious day in regard to Vishṇu), *paurṇami* (full moon day), *ashṭami* (the eighth day of waxing or waning moon), and birth day (of himself)," (*ĀK* 43), thus *Ācārakkōvai* very clearly endorses of canons of Vedic Hinduism and candidly restricts the man. If anyone violates this norm, it is believed that he/she will not experience any progress in his/her life. Interestingly, the ancient Tamiḻ *aham* ('love') poetry specifically identified the *naḻyāmam* (midnight, i.e., from 10 p.m. to 2 a.m.) as the most appropriate time for experiencing blissful sexual union. Nevertheless, this very time slot is categorized as inauspicious in certain orthodox traditions, during which sexual intercourse is discouraged. Aside from this particular period, other auspicious days and time frames may still carry some perceived validity or rational basis worth considering. Further, the *ĀK* strongly forbids in this regard by saying, the *pērarivāḷar* (the highly knowledgeable men), 'the great learned men' not only avoid having sex with their wives during their three days menstruation period but also would avoid looking at their face" (*ĀK* 42). From a hygiene perspective, as emphasized by the medical world, certain restrictions during menstruation are understandable. However, it is disheartening that some traditions go so far as to forbid men from even seeing the faces of their wives during this period. While such restrictions may seem excessive or even absurd, there could be an underlying rationale. If a man is highly driven by his ID, even a passionate glance at his wife might lead to sexual activity during this time, which could pose potential health risks. Interestingly, after this three-day restriction, the Vedic ethical text permits a man to engage in uninterrupted sexual pleasure with his wife for twelve consecutive days (*Ibid.*). This allowance is, in fact, a welcome shift—almost resembling a sound recommendation from a modern gynaecologist for a woman seeking sexual pleasure without the intention of conceiving.

*Ācāram*s (Virtuous Acts) of *Cāṉṟōr* (Noble Men)

The world indeed comprises countless beings beyond our imagination. In every being, good and bad elements do co-exist from evolution. In humankind, there exist simultaneously different categories—kings, justices, nobles, teachers, learned, farmers, traders, warriors, wrestlers, musicians, singers, dancers, illiterates, pimps, prostitutes, thieves, thugs, beggars, and what not—evolved on the basis of environment, education, knowledge, profession, character, and so on. Humans beings, in a sense, are really fortunate. When non-human beings allegedly can't learn good or bad attributes in systematic manners from their fellow beings, humans can have knowledge/wisdom and guidance on every matter from their elders. Out of the experience-cum-knowledge or wisdom, the erudite men talked about and chalked out certain rules and regulations, conventions and values and so on for leading life in a way beneficial to him and society. It is because of the intelligence, prudence and exemplary characteristics of prevailing nobles/wise men the world till date exists—though had seen and has been seeing numerous downfalls. The characteristics attributed to noble men do naturally vary from time to time, from culture to culture and from creed to creed. The men who led the life strictly as per the injunctions of Vedic *Śāstras* are hailed as noble men/wise men/ great men or prodigious men. "*Tirappaṭṭār* (the men of wisdom) do feel the pain of fellow men as their own. When fellow humans live cheerful, these people would indulge in such activities to make them further merry" (*ĀK* 79). "Even when they become annoyed, these great men—*don't call names* of their elders including their parents; *don't rebuke* them improperly; *don't abuse* even *pulaiyar* (outcaste men) by derogatory terms; *don't stay* at a place when they become angry with their wives" (*ĀK* 80). These well-mannered men would be very conscious enough where and how they should behave with other people. These people would never do anything that brings bad reputation to their family/ clan. So, "The *tirappaṭṭār* (the men of wisdom) *don't enter* the homes of loveless people" (*ĀK* 79). Further, "these *cevviyār* (the noble men) *don't enter* anybody's home through backyard; *don't visit* the king—when the monarch was in his private chamber or bedroom with his queen" (*ĀK* 81). The well-cultured people *don't tom-tom* their self-pride. This is one of their fine attributes. So, "they *don't talk* about the favours that they render to others. They *don't talk* praising their charity extended to people and they *don't glorify* their *nōṉbu* (the ritualistic observance or fasting) observed by them. These men of gratitude *don't complain* about the food that was offered to them by others" (*ĀK* 88). These *meyyāya kāṭciyavar* (the true visionaries), the men of wisdom *don't desire* for the improbable things; *don't worry* for the loss of wealth; *don't lose* their heart even when miseries ceaselessly engulf them" (*ĀK* 89). They strongly believe that everything happens by at the will of fate. So, they tend to take everything in good spirits. Subsequently, they just believe that if they worship their deity with utmost devotion and perform certain atonements sincerely then everything will be alright. So, they used to carry out certain rituals in this regard for welfare and benefits. "These wise men *don't live* near the brothel houses of prostitutes" (*ĀK* 82). "The men who earnestly care for their reputation—*don't look* at the burning light of thunderbolt and the down falling star; also, they *don't look* at the beautiful decoration of whores. And they *don't look* at even the beaming rays of the sun in the morning and self-effacing light of the same in the evening" (*ĀK* 51). Based on the etymological meaning of the Tamil term *nōkkār* ("those who do not look at something or someone") as used in the verse, we can understand that casually *seeing* something is not considered *unethical*. However, gazing intently or with desire is regarded as *immoral*. Even if a man does not become physically corrupt, he can still be mentally or spiritually polluted by such a look. When one's body gets polluted, it can be cleaned in a short time. When his mind gets infected, it will be next to impossible to get back the name lost out of infested action. So, "these *naḍukkaṟṟa kāṭciyar* ("the visionaries of unwavering mind"), "the resolute men of wisdom" *don't look at* women when they pound or husk something put into *ulakkai* (the long and heavy wooden pestle used traditionally in villages for pounding or husking paddy, ragi, etc.), and also they *don't go* to the home where a woman lives alone" (*ĀK* 99). "Besides, these men *don't look* at kitchen room either" (*Ibid.*). As these resolute men are very shrewd too, "they *don't go* to the melancholy places like gambling spot, and locations where *hulla gulla* is in roaring gear. If they go, then sure they will get a volume of miseries" (*ĀK* 98). Thus, *Ācārakkōvai* unveils a volume of ethical as well as unethical deeds that men need to adhere to for the sake of honorable life.

Aṉācārams (Non-Virtuous Acts)

Besides endorsing almost, a whole lot of *dharma*s inscribed in *Dharmaśāstra*s, the ethical treatise *Ācārakkōvai* also ratifies some sacrilegious *adharma*s or *aṉācāram*s that one should be aware of and stay away from those unethical activities. The thesis of ethical discourse is that if a person desires to have a fortunate life, he should tread the path of nobles. He should revere them on par with God whenever he encounters them. "When a man wishes to convey something to great men/ elders, first he should pay his respect to them. Then keeping his mouth covered by palm he should express obediently in low voice whatever he wishes to" (*ĀK* 97). A man should refrain from yelling at anyone—whether they are elders or noble individuals or even those who are younger or of lesser mind—especially if they have already passed by. And the person should also elude himself from sneezing, enquiring about the people's endpoint of their journey. Further, he should avoid interrupting and expressing something to them in the middle of the way" (*ĀK* 58). If the person disobeys, then all these become *aṉācāram*s (non-virtuous acts or bad behaviours) as per the view of *ĀK*. Cultured people do evade themselves from showing undue interest in several things. "They *don't ask* anyone—be he/she the priest, *guru*, mother, father, elder brother, nobles or *pulaiya*s even—about the food items that they have taken" (*ĀK* 86). This is an uncultured act, according to the ethical text. The text while ratifying the Vedic ethics' primary notion of "purity *vs.* impurity" observes, *"No one should wash* the feet of a person, *should not garland* him/her and more notably they *should not* at any cost *smear* sandal paste. And they *should not stand* near them" (*ĀK* 87). We can perceive the analogy here as a subtle reference to the customary decorations performed for the deceased. Traditionally, when a person passes away, people gather at the location, wash the feet of the deceased, apply sandal paste to the forehead, and adorn the body with garlands. These rituals, when symbolically imitated by a living person lying on a cot, are considered inauspicious and therefore become taboo. "A lady (a dignified woman) ought to avoid wearing the flowers worn and smelt by others" (*ĀK* 90). Noticeably, the versifier Kayattūr Peruvāyiṉ Muḷḷiyār validates the sanctity whatsoever assigned to flowers by the orthodox Vedic Hinduism in culture sphere.

Svarg (Heaven)–*Narak* (Hell): *Ācāram*s (Virtuous Acts)

Every creed immensely believes that somewhere above the sky exists 'the abode of Gods' or 'the world of Celestials' housing the *svarg* (heaven)–*narak* (hell) halls within. All religions systematically elucidate about these halls, of course, in different terms. In the context of India, the Vedic religion puts forward the thesis that there exists 'the Primordial Deity' or 'the Absolute Power' from which all the 'Creatures' or 'Beings' have materialized. Thus, 'the Creatures' or 'Beings' are, in fact, considered as the manifestations of that 'Supreme Power.' These 'entities of Created' have to return to 'the abode of the Creator' ultimately after experiencing the provisional life on the earth for some period. The Vedic faith further reiterates that the heaven or hell is actually accorded to *jīva*s (souls, i.e., all beings) on the basis of their *nalvinaigal* (good deeds) and *tīvinaigal* (bad deeds) carried out during the interim existence on earth. If human beings discharge upright deeds, certainly they could accomplish the *mukti/moksha* or *svarg*. Though Jainism also endorses this very notion of achieving *svarg* by one's righteous actions but discards the conception of God as it firmly hails the concept of "Perfect souls" existence on higher plane. Contrary to these faiths, Buddhism out rightly rejects whatsoever the views on Godhead and 'the Perfect Souls.' It is the "Sangha" (Assembly or Community) of Atheism juxtaposed to the Vedic religion on every matter, whereas closer to Jainism on emphasizing the righteous conduct for human beings.

According to Vedic and Jaina philosophies, stealing and enjoying others' belongings/properties are colossal wicked acts. It is unfortunate that in these two religions, women—the living human beings—were also grouped under the category of one's properties. "Adultery (covertly enjoying other man's wife), drinking toddy/liquor, stealing, gambling and killing are *pañca māpāthaka*s (the five gravest sins), thus *ĀK* (verse 37) approves the views of *Dharmaśāstra*s in toto. It is a firm conviction of Vedic faith that these gravest sins are being executed only by lower class people. *Ācārakkōvai*, the ethical text echoing openly the belief of the orthodox religion affirms, "The *aranarindār* (the men mindful of *dharma*s), 'the virtuous men' would never think of committing such sinful acts. If they think so, they would be derided as the men lacking noble ethos. Besides the wicked people would ultimately end up reaching the *nirayam* (hell)" (*Ibid.*). The orthodox ethical treatise similarly further asserts, "the *aiyamtīr kāṭciyar* (the visionaries of doubts be cleared), 'the resolute men of wisdom' wouldn't think of uttering lie and indulge in backbiting, wouldn't steal and become envy. If they think so, doubts over their piety will enter into the minds of people, and they will certainly reach hell. Sadly, even God will become angry and forsake them!" (*ĀK* 38). Thus, the text fully endorses the codes of Brāhmaṇism in both letter and spirit. While it may be beneficial for a higher ethical life, it also frightens humanity by asserting that people would reach hell even for common behaviours such as lying and backbiting. If we assess the validity of the aforementioned factors pragmatically, considering the realities of the world then and now, we can imagine a grim situation where most people would likely be condemned to hell, far more than those who live on earth. It may be stated here that **the halls of 'Heaven' and 'Hell' do not really exist anywhere beyond our purview. The two-fold mansions are indeed present within us—in our feelings and behavioural conducts of our daily life**. **Evidently, heaven or hell indeed is not a place but a state of feeling or consciousness that humans only can accomplish by adhering sincerely to certain basic ethical codes and practices endorsed by their nobles.** So, it is up to each individual to make or break heaven or hell. Essentially, everyone should adhere genuinely to the core etiquette and ethos of their society wherein they live for his/her happiness and that of fellow beings. Perhaps, in the quest for shepherding humans in the righteous path, the *Dharmaśāstra*s and *Ācārakkōvai* reiterated the aforesaid abstract forts, viz. 'Heaven' and 'Hell' by employing the typical strategy of 'reward' or 'punishment' to people's virtuous conducts and evil deeds respectively.

To sum up, the *ācāram*s and *aṉācāram*s—to be firmly adhered to by every traditional man from sleeping to salvation—are basically ritualistic but not very realistic by nature. Whatsoever observed ceremonially could not be said comprising the actual spirit or zeal/liveliness. **Can spiritless observances be called as *ācāram*s? Waking up, bathing, dressing, eating, sleeping, and engaging in sex—do all these actions need to be performed ritually or realistically? Does such mechanical action lead to *moksha*? No! Not at all! For that matter, no act should ever be performed ceremoniously—be it eating or excreting, sleeping or waking up, working or worshipping.** When the scriptures of bygone eras insist that man observe certain traditional codes and practices, there may indeed be rationality, logic, or scientific reasoning behind their pronouncements. However, what is most important above all is their applicability and adaptability. **Expecting everyone, including the under-privileged who struggle hard daily from hand to mouth with very little sources—to observe all orthodox codes and practices in the name of religious custom, is next to impractical and irrational. However, one should not excuse himself/herself but should observe and upheld certain very basic ethics or fundamental virtuous codes resolutely to the possible extent for the benefit of an individual and for the welfare of society.**

Notes

* This essay is the English version of my paper titled "Uṟakkam Mudal Tuṟakkam Varai: Ācāra-Aṉācāraṅgaḷ" (in Tamiḻ) presented in the National Seminar titled *Padiṉeṉ Kīḻkkaṇakku Nūlgaḷil Kaḍamaigaḷum Urimaigaḷum* (*Duties and Rights Stated in Eighteen Didactic Works*), sponsored by Central Institute of Classical Tamiḻ, Chennai, held at P.S.G. Krishnammal Women's College, Coimbatore, Tamiḻ Nadu during 11–13, February 2010.

1. *Padiṉeṉ Kīḻkkaṇakku Nūlgaḷ* (Eighteen Didactic Works): *Tirukkuṟaḷ, Nāladiyār, Palamoḻi Nāṉūṟu, Nāṉmaṇikkaḍigai, Iṉiyavai Nāṟpadu, Iṉṉā Nāṟpadu, Kār Nāṟpadu, Kaḷavaḻi Nāṟpadu, Tirikaḍugam, Ācārakkōvai, Ciṟupañcamūlam, Mudumoḻikkāñci, Ēlādi, Tiṇaimoḻi Aimbadu, Aintiṇai Aimbadu, Aintiṇai Eḻubadu, Tiṇaimālai Nūṟṟaimbadu, Kainnilai.*

2. *Ācārakkōvai* is an ethical work included in the compilation of the Eighteen Didactic Tamiḻ Works called "Padiṉeṉ Kīḻkkaṇakku Nūlgaḷ." Its title literally means "the garland of moral codes." Its author Kayattūr Peruvāyiṉ Muḷḷiyār of Śaiva faith seems to be highly influenced by Vedic *Śāstras* and tenets of Hinduism. There is heavy dosage of Brahminical influence in a number of verses. Hence, it is considered to be the ethical work composed in the later period of post-Sangam Age, i.e., 800 CE. The ethical work has 100 poems in *veṇpā* meter and is a collection of moral exhortations, ritual observances and customs that are considered so proper and correct for everyone. The injunctions endorsed in the stanzas of *Ācārakkōvai* are concerned with personal rituals, morals, etiquettes, taboos and the proper methods to follow in day today life.

3. Please see the reference cited in the foot no. 4, Chapter: One.

4. *Aham* means "interior emotions" (mostly of women) such as sexual union, sulking, separation, waiting with patience, and waiting with anxiety. It also refers to "heart" and "household" in Tamiḻ diction. *Akam* poems are love poems.

5. *Puṟam* means "exterior actions" (largely of men) such as dignity, valour, munificence, mourning, and so on. *Puṟam* poems are all other kinds of poems, usually about war, values, community; it is the "public" poetry of the ancient Tamiḻs, celebrating the ferocity and glory of kings, lamenting the death of heroes, poems on wars and tragic events are *puṟam* poems.

6. *Varṇa*, a Sanskrit term literally means "colour." It is derived from the root *vrnoti* meaning 'to cover' or 'to envelop.' The word finds its first mention in the *Rig Veda* where it stands for 'outer appearance and colour' besides the figurative "race, colour, kind, sort, character, quality." As detailed in *Manusmriti* (Laws

of Manu), (200 BCE–200 CE), the earliest metrical work of the *Dharmaśāstra*s, The *Varṇa* system as laid down in the religious texts right from the *Rig Veda* to the *Manusmriti* was based on four hierarchically arranged *Varṇa*s, viz. *Brāhmiṇ*s, *Kshatriya*s, *Vaishya*s and *Shūdra*s with the *Avarṇa*s (Untouchables) placed at the bottom of hierarchy.

Source: http://www.ijelr.in/2.1.15/237-239%20RICHA%20SHARMA.
     pdf

As per the citations of *Manusmriti*, people of the four *Varṇa*s are believed to have born to the Brahman, the Almighty from His mouth, arms, thighs, and feet respectively. See the *Sloka*s of *Manusmriti* given below:

"But for the sake of the prosperity of the worlds he caused the *Brahmana*, the *Kshatriya*, the *Vaisya*, and the *Sudra* to proceed from his mouth, his arms, his thighs, and his feet" (*Manu Smriti* 1.31).

"But in order to protect this universe He, the most resplendent one, assigned separate (duties and) occupations to those who sprang from his mouth, arms, thighs, and feet" (*Manu Smriti* 1.87).

Source: https://www.quora.com/Vedic-Hinduism-Why-did-Manu-
     Smriti-created-four-varna-system-and-looks-Shudras-so-
     low-Why-didnt-the-ancient-scholars-oppose-it

7.   Source: https://ta.wikipedia.org/wiki/கொன்றை வேந்தன்

8.   *Gurukula* (Sanskrit: *Gurukul*) is a type of residential school in India with pupils (*shishya*) living near the *guru*, often in the same house. Before British rule, they served as South Asia's primary educational institution. The *guru-shishya* tradition (*parampara*) is a hallowed one in Hinduism and appears in other religious groups in India, such as Jainism, Buddhism, and Sikhism. The word *gurukula* is a contraction of the Sanskrit *guru* (teacher or master) and *kula* (extended family).

In a *gurukula, shishya* live together as equals, irrespective of their social standing, learn from the *guru* and help the *guru* in his day-to-day life, including the carrying out of mundane chores such as washing clothes, cooking, etc. Typically, a *guru* does not receive any fees from the *shishya* studying with him. At the end of his studies, a *shishya* offers the *guru dakshina* before leaving the *gurukula* or *ashram*. The *gurudakshina* is a traditional gesture of acknowledgment, respect and thanks to the *guru*, which may be monetary, but may also be a special task the teacher wants the student to accomplish. While living in a *gurukula* the students had to be away from home and family completely. The *guru* did not take any fees and so they had to serve the *guru*.

Gurukula have existed since the Vedic age. *Upanishad*s mention many *gurukula*, including that of *guru* Drona at Gurugram, Yajnavalkya, Varuni. Bhrigu Valli, the famous discourse on Brahman, is mentioned to have taken place in Guru Varuni's *gurukula*. Vedic school of thought prescribes an initiation (*Upanayana*, a compulsory *Sanskara* or activity for a Hindu living) to all individuals before the age of 8 or latest by 12. From initiation until the age of 25 all individuals are prescribed to be students and to remain unmarried.

Source: https://en.wikipedia.org/wiki/Gurukula

9. Enlightenment refers to the "full comprehension of a situation" … It translates several Buddhist terms and concepts, most notably *Bodhi, Kensho* and *Satori*. Related terms from Asian religions are *Moksha* (liberation) in Hinduism, *Kevala Jnana* in Jainism, and *Ushta* in Zoroastrianism.

    In Christianity, the word "enlightenment" is rarely used, except to refer to the Age of Enlightenment and its influence on Christianity. Roughly equivalent terms in Christianity may be illumination, kenosis, metanoia, revelation, salvation and conversion.

    The English term "enlightenment" has commonly been used to translate several Sanskrit, Pali, Chinese and Japanese terms and concepts, especially *bodhi, prajna, kensho, satori* and *Buddhahood*.

    Bodhi is a *Theravada* term. It literally means "awakening" and "understanding." Someone who is awakened has gained insight into the workings of the mind which keeps us imprisoned in craving, suffering and rebirth, and has also gained insight into the way that leads to nirvana, the liberation of oneself from this imprisonment.

Prajna is a *Mahayana* term. It refers to insight into our true nature, which according to *Madhyamaka* is empty of a personal essence in the stream of experience. But it also refers to the *Tathāgata-garbha* or Buddha-nature, the essential basic-consciousness beyond the stream of experience.

In Indian religions *moksha* (*mokṣa*, 'liberation') or *mukti* (release – both from the root *muc* "to let loose, let go") is the final extrication of the soul or consciousness (*purusha*) from *samsara* and the bringing to an end of all the suffering involved in being subject to the cycle of repeated death and rebirth (reincarnation).

Source: https://en.wikipedia.org/wiki/Enlightenment_(spiritual)

10. *Atithi*: "The word *atithi* is from the root *'at'* to go and also from *tithi* (day) and *'a'* meaning comes (from *'ī'* with *abhi*). [...] Manu and others say that for a whole *tithi* (i.e., day) and 'an *atithi*' is a *brāhmaṇa* who stays for one night only as a guest" (Kane 1941: 751). *Dharmasutra* of Gauthama V. 36, Manu III. 102–103 and *Yajñavalkyasmṛti* I. 107 state that he is called an *atithi* who belonging to a different village and intending to stay one night only arrives in the evening, that one who has already been invited for dinner is not an *atithi* properly so called, that a person who belongs to the same village or who is a friend or fellow-student is not an *atithi*" (Kane, *Ibid.*).

    Cf.: Pandurang Vaman Kane. 1941. *History of Dharmasastra*. Vol. II, Part II. Poona: Bhandarkar Oriental Research Institute. pp. 149–152.

11. Under the *Ashram* system, human life was divided into four periods. The goal of each period was the fulfillment and development of the individual. While some Indian texts present these as sequential stages of human life and recommend age when one enters each stage, many texts state that the *Āshrama*s as four alternative ways of life and options available, but not as sequential stage that any individual must follow, nor do they place any age limits.

The *Āshrama* System

Ashram or stage	Age (years)	Description	Rituals of transition
Brahma-charya (Student life)	Till 24 years	*Brahmacharya* represented the bachelor student stage of life. This stage focused on education and included the practice of celibacy. The student went to a *Gurukul* (house of the *Guru*) and typically would live with a *Guru* (teacher), acquiring knowledge of science, philosophy, scriptures and logic, practicing self-discipline, working to earn *dakshina* to be paid for the *guru*, learning to live a life of Dharma (righteousness, morals, duties).	*Upanayana* at entry. *Samavartana* at exit.
Grihastha (House holder life)	From 24 to 48 years	This stage referred to the individual's married life, with the duties of maintaining a household, raising a family, educating one's children, and leading a family-centred and a dharmic social life. *Grihastha* stage was considered as the most important of all stages in sociological context, as human beings in this stage not only pursued a virtuous life, they produced food and wealth that sustained people in other stages of life, as well as the offspring that continued mankind. The stage also represented one where the most intense physical, sexual, emotional, occupational, social and materal attachments exist in a human being's life.	Hindu Wedding at entry.

Vana-prastha (Retired life)	From 48 to 72 years	The retirement stage, where a person handed over household responsibilities to the next generation, took an advisory role, and gradually withdrew from the world. *Vānaprastha* stage was a transition phase from a householder's life with its greater emphasis on *Artha* and *Kāma* (wealth, security, pleasure and sexual pursuits) to one with greater emphasis on *Moksha* (spiritual liberation).	
Sannyasa (Renounced life)	From 72 onwards (or any time)	The stage was marked by renunciation of material desires and prejudices, represented by a state of disinterest and detachment from material life, generally without any meaningful property or home (Ascetic), and focused on *Moksha*, peace and simple spiritual life. Anyone could enter this stage after completing the *Brahmacharya* stage of life.	

Source: https://en.wikipedia.org/wiki/Ashrama_(stage)
Accessed on 28th August 2016.

References

Acarya, Dr. C.R. (tr.). 1999. *Maxims of Truth*. Tiruttani: C.R. Acharya Publication.

Bharati, Yogi Shuddhananda. 2008. (3rd ed.). *Thirukkural With Couplets*. Chennai: Shree Shenbhaga Pathippagam.

Dikshitar, Prof. V.R. Ramachandra. (tr.). 1978. *The Cilappatikaram*. Chennai: The South India Saiva Siddhanta Works Publishing Society.

Drew, Rev. W. H. & Rev. John Lazarus (trs.). 1989. (IInd Rpt). *Thirukkural*. New Delhi: Asian Educational Services.

Gopala Krishnamachariyar, Vai.Mu. (comm.). 1965. *Śrī Kamba Rāmāyaṇam* (in Tamiḻ). Chennai: Vai.Mu. Krishnamachariyar Company.

.... 1965 (IVth ed.). *Kamba Rāmāyaṇam – Āraṇya Kāṇḍam* (in Tamiḻ). Chennai: Kuvai Publications.

.... 1965. *Śrī Kamba Rāmāyaṇam – Bāla Kāṇḍam* (in Tamiḻ). Chennai: Kuvai Publication.

Hart, George L. & Hank Heifetz. (trs.). 1999. *The Four Hundred Songs of War and Wisdom*. New York: Columbia University Press.

Ilakkuvanar, Prof. S. 1963. *Tholkāppiyam (in English) with Critical Studies*. Madurai: Kural Neri Publishing House.

Ilampuranar. (comm.). 1981 (Rpt.). *Tolkāppiyam – Colladigāram* (in Tamiḻ). Chennai: South India Saiva Siddhanta Works Publishing Society.

.... 1982 (Rpt.). *Tolkāppiyam – Poruḷa-digāram* (in Tamiḻ). Chennai: South India Saiva Siddhanta Works Publishing Society.

Ilango Adigal. 1985. *Cilappadigāram* (in Tamiḻ). Tanjavur: Tamil University.

Indira, C.T. (tr.). 2003. *The Legend of Nandaṉ – Nandaṉ Kathai.* New Delhi: Oxford University Press.

Kane, Pandurang Vaman. 1930. *History of Dharmasastra.* Vol. I, Part I. Poona: Bhandarkar Oriental Research Institute.

.... 1941. *History of Dharmasastra.* Vol. II, Part I. Poona: Bhandarkar Oriental Research Institute.

.... 1941. *History of Dharmasastra.* Vol. II, Part II. Poona: Bhandarkar Oriental Research Institute.

.... 1946. *History of Dharmasastra.* Vol. III, Part I. Poona: Bhandarkar Oriental Research Institute.

Kathiraiverpillai, Na. 1984 (6th corrected ed.). *Tamiḻ Moḻi-yagarādi* (in Tamiḻ). New Delhi: Asian Educational Services.

Manavalan, A.A. 1990. "Didactic Literature in Tamil," In *Encyclopadia of Tamil Literature.* Dr. G. John Samuel (ed.). Madras: Institute of Asian Studies.

Parthasarathy, R. 1993. *The Cilappatikaram of Ilanko Atikal.* New York: Columbia University Press.

Peruvayin Mulliyar, Kayattur. 1971. (Ist ed. 1939). *Padiṉeṉ Kīḻk-kaṇakku—Kāñci, Ēlādi, Kōvai* (in Tamiḻ). P.C. Punnaivanana-tha Mudaliyar (Viruttiyurai). Chennai: Tirunelveli South India Saiva Siddhanta Works Publishing House.

Ponniah, Prof. S.M. (tr.). 1997. *Tamil Poetry Through Ages*. Vol. I. Dr. G. Samuel & Dr. Shu Hikosaka (General Eds.). Chennai: Institute of Asian Studies.

Pope, Rew. G.U. & F.W. Ellis. (trs.). 1958. *Naladiyar*. Chennai: The South India Saiva Siddhanta Works Publishing Society.

.... (tr.). 1984 (Rpt). *The Nalatiyar* (*Four Hundred Quatrains in Tamiḻ*). New Delhi: Asian Educational Services.

Rajagopal, G. 2007. *Beyond Bhakti: Steps Ahead* ... New Delhi: B.R. Publishing Corporation.

Raj Gauthaman. 1997. *Aram/Adhikaram* (in Tamiḻ). Kovai (Coimbatore): Vidiyal Pathippagam.

Ramanujan, A. K. 1985. *Poems of Love and War*. Delhi: Oxford University Press.

.... 2006 (3rd Impn.). *The Collected Essays of A.K. Ramanujan*. New Delhi: Oxford University Press.

Seshadri, K.G. (tr.). 1996. *Paripatal*. Dr. M. Shanmugam Pillai & Dr. P. Thiagarajan (Eds.). Chennai: Institute of Asian Studies.

Sundaram, P.S. (tr.). 1991. *Kamba Ramayanam – Aranya Kandam*. Chennai: Department of Tamil Development – Culture.

Vaiyapurippillai. S. (ed.). 1967 (IInd ed.). *Canga Ilakkiyam – Pāṭṭum Tokaiyum* (in Tamiḻ). Vol. I & II. Chennai: Pari Nilaiyam.

.... 1982 (Rpt.). *Tamil Lexicon*. Vol. III. Madras: University of Madras.

.... 1982 (Rpt.). *Tamil Lexicon*. Vol. IV. Part I. Chennai: University of Madras.

Varadarajanar, Mu. 1974 (26th Impn., I[st] ed. 1949). *Tirukkuṟaḷ Teḷivurai* (in Tamiḻ). Chennai: South India Saiva Siddhanta Works Publishing Society.

Vishwanathan, Pulavar R. 2011. *THIRUKKURAL – Universal Tamil Scripture*. Mumbai: Bharatiya Vidya Bhavan.

Zvelebil, Kamil V. 1973. *The Smile of Murugan*. Leiden: E. J. Brill.

.... 1974. *Tamil Literature*. Wiesbaen: Otto Harras-sowitz.

Index

About the Author

Govindaswamy Rajagopal (b. 1960 –) is a Professor who teaches Tamil and Comparative Indian Literature in the Department of Modern Indian Languages and Literary Studies at the University of Delhi since 1987 and served as the Head of the Department for three years (2017–2020). He earned his PhD by critically analysing the structure of *mudal* (basic elements), *karu* (native elements) and *uri* (love themes) in *Ahanāṉūṟu* under the guidance of eminence Tamiḻ scholars, Prof. Tamiḻaṇṇal (Rama. Periya Karuppan) and Prof. Pon. Sourirajan. He has also served as the Visiting Professor of Tamil in the Department of Indology, Institute of Oriental Studies, Jagiellonian University, Krakow, Poland for two academic years (2011–2013) and as the Programme External Examiner for Bachelor of Arts in Tamil Language and Literature programme for the Singapore University of Social Sciences (SUSS), Singapore for three academic years (2017–2020).

Besides this book, Rajagopal has authored four books in English titled *Beyond Bhakti: Steps Ahead...* (2007), *Mind and Conduct: Behavioural Psychology in the Sangam Poetry* (2015), *Cultural Poetics and Sangam Poetry* (2016), and *Re-reading of Classical Tamiḻ Literary Works: Chronicles of Ancient Tamiḻs' Life* (2021) and one book in Tamiḻ titled *Kāmaṉ Kadaippāḍal: Ōr Āyvu* (*The Ballad on Kama: A Study*), (1986). He has presented nearly fifty research papers on various themes at National and International Conferences held in Malaysia, Poland, Czech, France and the USA. Various reputed Research Institutions and Universities in India and abroad have published his research papers focused on *Sangam*, *Tirukkuṟaḷ*, and *Bhakti* literature.